PRAISE FOR
CARNIVORE LEADERSHIP

"From the moment I met 'CZ' Colón-López, I knew he was someone I wanted on my team. He has such a deep knowledge of so many subjects, but he is blessed with a humility that belies his vast life experience—experience that took him from some of the most dangerous combat zones on earth to the very highest corridors of power. In other words, CZ is not the kind of person who will ever tell you that he knows more than you or has done more than you. He doesn't have to. That's the thing about great leaders who have walked the walk. For men like CZ, boasting is pointless. Men like this communicate with such surety and clarity that their capabilities are self-evident. So when CZ told me he was writing a leadership book, my expectations were sky-high. *Carnivore Leadership*, naturally, exceeds all of them and offers readers the chance to do the very same and very wise thing that I did some years ago: welcome CZ into your life and heed his advice. It's made me a better person and can do the same for you."

—**Chef Robert Irvine,** entrepreneur and philanthropist

"*Carnivore Leadership* is a great and easy read for anyone serious about self-improvement and the art of leadership. I've known CZ for years, working with him during the toughest of times at the Pentagon. The stories he tells are not just insightful; they reflect the leader he is—interesting, authentic, and inspiring."

—**Dr. Mark T. Esper,** twenty-seventh US Secretary of Defense

"I was blessed with great leaders in both pararescue and the CIA, and I learned by their example. However, most readers will not have access to this mentorship I enjoyed. That is why I highly recommend *Carnivore Leadership*. CZ has led several generations of warfighters and groomed them for success—and survival. Whether in a kinetic mission or clinching a corporate contract, CZ would be my go-to guy. Even now, I learned a bit more via this wonderful book."

—**Ric Prado,** *New York Times* bestselling author of *Black Ops*, CIA Senior Operations Officer, and Chief of Operations at CIA's Counterterrorist Center (Retired)

"SEAC Ramón Colón-López embodies leadership in every sense of the word. In a world crowded with leadership buzzwords and empty slogans, CZ delivers the real thing: raw, honest, and forged through decades of experience where lives, missions, and trust were on the line. This isn't theory—it's battle-tested truth with hard-earned lessons that apply whether you lead on the battlefield, in the boardroom, or anywhere in between. If you're serious about leading with purpose, resilience, and clarity, this book will challenge you to take charge—and get to work."

—**Matthew O. Williams,** Medal of Honor recipient

"SEAC Ramón Colón-López has always led with integrity, grit, and purpose—and this book is no different. It cuts through the noise and delivers real leadership lessons forged through decades of service at the highest levels. No fluff, no ego—just the truth from someone who has lived it. A must-read for anyone serious about leading. This book is a master class in leadership from one of the best to ever wear the uniform."

—**Flo Groberg,** Medal of Honor recipient

"As someone rescued by SEAL Team Six, I understand that missions like mine are only possible because of exceptional leadership behind the scenes. *Carnivore Leadership* is a powerful look into the mindset of those who lead from the front—decisively, humbly, and with unwavering integrity. Ramón 'CZ' Colón-López embodies what it means to take radical ownership and lead with purpose under pressure. His story is both inspiring and deeply instructive for anyone seeking to lead with clarity and courage. This book is a master class in action-oriented leadership that the world desperately needs right now."

—**Jessica Buchanan,** *New York Times* bestselling author of *Impossible Odds: The Kidnapping of Jessica Buchanan and Her Dramatic Rescue by SEAL Team Six*

"CZ is the kind of leader who doesn't just raise the bar—he redefines it, and this book shows you how he does it. There are few leaders I hold in the highest regard—SEAC Ramón Colón-López is one of them. He's the rare kind of man whose presence raises the performance of everyone around him, not by title but by the strength of his integrity, humility, and unwavering standards. This book isn't just a leadership guide—it's a blueprint forged by a warrior who's led with honor at the highest levels and continues to shape organizations and leaders into elite teams."

—**Mike Sarraille,** Navy SEAL (Retired) and Chief Talent Officer of Overwatch Mission Critical

"Ramón 'CZ' Colón-López is the embodiment of no-nonsense leadership. His words carry the weight of decades at the sharpest edge of global operations, and this book distills those hard-earned lessons into actionable truth. It's a must-read for anyone serious about leadership, accountability, and impact. I'm proud to support CZ and this mission."

—**Louis Skupien,** host of the *TALK4* podcast

"Together we recognize those who exemplify leadership and inspire us to become better. CZ is a man who will always strive to see and draw out the best in all who surround him. He will always put his first (best) step forward for others. He strives for greatness because he knows we must every day if we want to be and have the best opportunities our lives have to offer. Good people are our greatest assets that we try to hold on to as long as we can. CZ knows a commitment of our time for others is needed to grow relationships and a team. He's a true friend, one who will fight and defend you because you share common values and character, even when you don't share common ground. He embodies the word *trust* through his honesty and example. I highly recommend that any opportunity you get to read his words, you listen and learn. His experiences in life are vast but his time, like ours, is not infinite. Take the opportunity to be a better person or leader and learn what you can from a great example."

—**Leroy Petry,** MSG (Retired) and Medal of Honor recipient

"SEAC Ramón Colón-López is the definition of a warrior-leader. His integrity, humility, and relentless service to our nation's heroes set the bar for all of us. I've witnessed firsthand his dedication to our veterans and warriors, and I'm honored to stand behind him and this important work. This book will no doubt be a powerful guide for leaders who are ready to step up and lead with purpose."

—**Tom Satterly,** CSM (Retired), bestselling author, and founder of All-Secure Foundation

"The word *carnivore* is associated with predators who aggressively devour others using directed violence. *Carnivore* also connotes a kind of ruthlessness. Make no mistake. SEAC Ramón 'CZ' Colón-López is a warrior's warrior. But *Carnivore Leadership* is about a different kind of 'hunting capability' and a different kind of hunger. Colón-López calls to those who hunger for uncertainty, who crave opportunities to put themselves to the test, and those willing to make sacrifices others won't in the service of values they hold sacred. A carnivore without a moral compass is a dangerous psychopath. A carnivore who acts from the warrior's creed is a warrior for the ages. To appreciate the true meaning of a Carnivore leader, consider this example: when asked, 'How many people have you killed?' Colón-López instinctively responds, 'Wouldn't you be more interested in how many lives I've saved?' CZ lives out the value of self-sacrifice with a 'no-fail mindset' because 'falling short . . . could mean the inability to save someone's life, to bring them back home to their families, or not being ready when the call to danger came.' In my years of experience supporting our nation's elite warriors, I've seen that CZ sets the highest standards for leadership. He is ruthlessly self-determined to sharpen himself, and in so doing, to remind warriors of who they should be. *Carnivore Leadership* is a decisive answer to the mealy-mouthed advice promoted in other leadership books."

—**Shauna "Doc" Springer,** PhD, author of *Warrior* and *Relentless Courage*

"War is the ultimate competition. There is no respawn. It requires less theory and more application. Tactics, techniques, and procedures are relentlessly improved. CZ brings a 'lifestyle approach' to leadership and improvement. His ethos ensured our battlefield success!"

—**James J. Hintzke,** SOCM (Retired)

"*Carnivore Leadership* is a must-read for anyone serious about leveling up their leadership capabilities. Ramón Colón-López—a thirty-three-year veteran of the US Air Force—spent most of his career in elite special operations units, where leadership isn't about titles or rank, but about earning trust in the most high-stakes environments imaginable. Drawing from his front-line experience in the global war on terror, Colón-López delivers hard-won lessons that are as relevant in the boardroom as they are on the battlefield. *Carnivore Leadership* is equal parts inspirational and practical—a blueprint for those who want to lead with courage, conviction, and a sense of humor. I have the pleasure of working with Colón-López on several current projects and can attest that he 'walks the talk' of his leadership principles. It's no surprise he rose to become the highest-ranking enlisted service member in the US military, the SEAC. Now buckle up and get in the fight!"

—**Tom Davin,** US Marine Corps Infantry and Reconnaissance Officer, former co-CEO of Black Rifle Coffee Company, and CEO of 5.11 Tactical

"SEAC Ramón Colón-López doesn't just write about leadership; he lives it in every aspect of his life. Whether working on a business venture, handling his personal life, or enthusiastically supporting the military community, he attacks everything with relentless passion, drive, commitment, and no-nonsense leadership. Highly ethical and inspirational, Colón-López sets a personal leadership example for others to follow. No matter how long you've led or how many people, anyone who reads this book will find something of value."

—**Mark Steffe,** President/CEO of First Command Financial Services, Inc.

"Ray 'CZ' Colón-López is not just a warrior—he is a leader whose integrity, strength, and humility have lifted our nation's most sacred communities, including the grieving families of our fallen at TAPS. I've stood beside him as he's comforted survivors with quiet resolve and inspired action with fierce compassion. In *Carnivore Leadership*, CZ doesn't just teach us how to lead—he reminds us why we must. He speaks from the heart of experience, with wisdom forged on the battlefield and tested in the highest halls of power. This book is a rare and necessary gift: a raw, unflinching call to lead with moral courage, clarity of purpose, and service above self. It is the legacy of a leader who never backed down—and a road map for those bold enough to step up."

—**Bonnie Carroll,** President and Founder of Tragedy Assistance Program for Survivors (TAPS)

"Having had the distinct privilege of serving alongside CZ for over twenty years across multiple demanding assignments, I can attest to his exceptional leadership. Together, we tackled some of our nation's most complex challenges. I witnessed firsthand that he is an inspirational leader of character and integrity, a man of action, not just words, always holding himself to the highest standards as a humble professional. CZ didn't just write the words in this book; he lives by them every day. The principles and insights he shares are applicable at every level of leadership, from tactical to strategic, and are invaluable whether you are leading yourself or others. This book is a testament to the leader I know, and I wholeheartedly recommend it."

—**Jason France,** CMSgt (Retired); former CSEL, US Transportation Command; and author of *Five Million Steps: Hiking the Pacific Crest Trail after Three Decades of Service to Our Nation*

"*Carnivore Leadership* transcends military and industry. CZ brings out the best in everyone, cuts through distractions, and gets directly to what matters. I have experienced CZ's authentic and proactive leadership through a friendship that began thirty years ago as classmates in the Army Combat Diver Qualification Course. His leadership principles continue to impact those who serve and impact leaders in industry dedicated to supporting those who serve. CZ's lessons are a must for anyone committed to individual and team development with the self-awareness to know that you can never stop learning. If you do, you risk becoming irrelevant."

—**Ryan Angold,** CEO of ADS Inc.

"As a retired Tier 1 operator, I am honor-bound to defend the integrity and uphold the values of the SOF community— there's no room for valor merchants. CZ is the furthest thing from that. He is a man of unwavering character who shouldered our nation's call with uncommon resolve and humility. *Carnivore Leadership* reflects that same spirit, delivering raw, unfiltered truths about what it takes to lead with courage, conviction, and integrity. If you're serious about becoming a better human and leveling up your leadership skills, you need to consume this book."

—**Edward C. Byers Jr.,** Medal of Honor recipient and Navy SEAL Master Chief (Retired)

"CZ doesn't hand out leadership lessons—he drops battle-tested truth bombs. *Carnivore Leadership* is what happens when discipline, danger, and duty collide with purpose. This isn't for people looking for motivation—it's for those ready to move. If you've ever felt the pressure to lead without a playbook, this is what you need, straight from a man who has lived it, led it, and bled for it."

—**Mick Hunt,** the Voice of Modern Leadership and host of *Mick Unplugged*

"CZ is a humble, credible, approachable leader who brought calm to chaotic situations throughout his military career. He's the first in line to roll up his sleeves and get dirty. CZ never asked anyone to do something he wouldn't do himself and used his successes and failures to grow our next generation of military leaders. As you read *Carnivore Leadership*, you'll be immersed in CZ's lessons of how to lead with a pure heart and deliver a clear vision for your team, in the boardroom or on the battlefield. The fresh and inspiring lessons will give you a road map for creating a working environment where the men and women in your organization will feel a sense of purpose and pride. CZ is a fire-and-forget problem solver that *always* finds a way to yes. He answered the call and was the first in line to deliver solutions for the nation's hardest problems. During my thirty-two-year military career and over two decades in special operations, I had the privilege to serve alongside thousands of amazing men and women. CZ is absolutely one of the best. His fierce dedication to our people, our mission, and our country is evident in everything he touches. I've flown thousands of combat hours in the AC-130 SPECTRE and U-28 DRACO and witnessed missions not go as planned. When the shit hits the fan, you rely on quiet professionals like CZ to answer the call. He is a trusted operator and advisor whose passion is contagious. I'm proud to call him a friend."

—**Allison Black,** Colonel, US Air Force (Retired), a.k.a. Angel of Death; former Commander, 1st Special Operations Wing, Air Force Special Operations, Hurlburt Field, Florida

www.amplifypublishinggroup.com

Carnivore Leadership: Taking Charge Instead of Taking Shit

Second printing. This Amplify Publishing edition printed in 2026.

For more information, please contact:
Amplify Publishing, an imprint of Amplify Publishing Group
620 Herndon Parkway, Suite 220
Herndon, VA 20170
info@amplifypublishing.com

Library of Congress Control Number: 2025914039

CPSIA Code: PRV0326B

ISBN-13: 979-8-89138-655-6

Printed in the United States

This book is dedicated to my parents for allowing me to dream, my wife for allowing me to soar, and my teammates for always having my back.

CARNIVORE LEADERSHIP

TAKING CHARGE INSTEAD OF TAKING SHIT

RAMÓN COLÓN-LÓPEZ

CONTENTS

FOREWORD

As a commander in joint special operations, I had the honor to lead many remarkable American warfighters and leaders who took on our nation's toughest missions. These men and women were Americans who not only answered the call to service but also chose the most arduous crucibles to become our special operations forces. Our Air Force Special Tactics Pararescuemen are among those valiant few who dare go forth. These incredible warriors were my emergency fallback for complex rescue operations and my insurance policy for the survival of my Tier 1 forces.

Ramón "CZ" Colón-López spent his adult life in combat and leading at every level in the Department of Defense, culminating with his selection as the Senior Enlisted Advisor to the Chairman (SEAC) of the Joint Chiefs of Staff, the highest-ranking noncommissioned officer in the United States of America. I personally had the honor to lead CZ during our time in JSOC as he led our Special Tactics forces during some critical missions. His credibility transcends across the force as a tough, dependable, and loyal teammate that will not leave anything to chance.

A common attribute among many of our special operators is humility. They are never content, always seeking improvement. From lethality to leadership acumen, they are lifelong students of the art of warfare, and masters at translating those skills for all who can benefit from them. *Carnivore Leadership* is an example of this, and while the word "carnivore" evokes wild meat-eating animals hunting weak prey, CZ demonstrates the full scope of servant leadership in this unique approach to today's challenges.

Throughout his career, CZ championed "carnivore leadership," a term he attributes to Jim Hintzke, a Navy SEAL Master Chief and teammate from the early days in Afghanistan. This concept is rooted in the distinction between being proactive and assertive, akin to carnivores, as opposed to adopting a more passive, reactive stance likened to grass eaters. The metaphor perfectly encapsulates CZ's philosophy: it emphasizes the need for leaders to be decisively action-oriented, taking initiative rather than waiting for events to unfold. This style of leadership resonated deeply with the troops, who appreciated candid discussion about their roles and the conduct expected of them.

CZ embraced the carnivore model, finding that it aligned well with his own experiences and the dynamic demands of military leadership. This approach isn't just about being aggressive; it represents a broader spectrum of traits, including open-mindedness, humility, and honesty, balanced with the assertiveness and decisiveness characteristic of carnivores. His commitment to this style is reflected in his daily practice of documenting interactions and lessons learned, an exercise that has significantly sharpened his leadership acumen.

The essence of *Carnivore Leadership* lies in fostering a decisive, action-oriented, and operations-focused model. It's a leadership paradigm that encourages taking the lead, being at the forefront of challenges, and proactively seeking solutions. This perspective has not only been crucial in CZ's successful military career but also serves as a powerful example for leaders in all fields seeking to cultivate a more dynamic and impactful leadership style.

Ramón "CZ" Colón-López's extraordinary journey from poverty to the Pentagon is a master class in leadership and resilience. His life story offers profound lessons for men and women seeking to forge their path in today's complex world. As we reflect on CZ's narrative, it prompts us to ask: ***How can we apply the principles of humility, resilience, and moral courage in our lives? How can we, like CZ, transform our challenges into opportunities for growth and leadership?***

CZ is one of the finest leaders of our time, and it is my honor to have served with him. You, the reader, will gain incredible insights from this remarkable book. Start your new leadership journey now.

—William H. McRaven
Admiral, US Navy (Retired)

PROLOGUE

There are words and phrases you'll never hear from the mouth of a warrior, like "fabulous" or "cute" (unless being pointedly sarcastic), or "pearls of wisdom." In keeping with the carnivore warrior mindset, one of my trusted mentors pointed out that "pearls of wisdom" are for the weak, and that the term itself sounded soft. So I chose Silver Bullets instead. A bullet hits a target and makes an impact, and the Silver Bullets in this book will make an impact too. They will help forge courageous leadership, inspire confidence, and evoke thoughts that spark action.

In 2012, during my first leadership tour as a Command Senior Enlisted Leader, Janet and I decided to draft a leadership development paper based on a collection of quotes I had accumulated during my time as a Joint Special Operations Command (JSOC) Tier 1 operator. Janet was keen on developing something different, what the masses—or more specifically my leadership peers—were afraid to say. She reflected on the many times she had heard leaders give canned speeches that were nothing more than lip service. The common "blah blah blah" approach to leadership communication needed to be challenged, broken, and changed.

With that in mind, the purpose of the paper was to instill an aggressive approach to experiential learning and courageous action, much like my time in special ops. Coupled with Janet's assessment of her own experiences serving in the military, the main driver for the release of Volume 1 of the paper was the inadequacies of past leaders and their disconnection from the issues that affected people the most. While those leaders played it safe and avoided making waves, we needed to step up and speak in the voice of the people. So I spent the first ninety days of my assignment talking to people across the organization, gathering feedback on their issues and the leadership actions they expected from the commander and me. The original paper, drafted for a specific military audience, appears in an Appendix at the end of this book.

I chose the title *Carnivore Leadership* while comparing "meat eaters" to "grass eaters" in a culture of war fighting. The paper was well received by most of the organization, not just the intended military audience. As with anything in life, it was a bit too aggressive for some. A few even found it offensive, mainly because they were guilty of some of the behaviors the paper sought to eliminate. Others mentioned the "omnivore" dilemma, a compromise or balance between the two entities, not too aggressive and not too passive.

I chose to stick with the two extremes, partly because I saw what was coming from those who sought an in-between. They wanted to stay in the status quo of their comfort zone. They wanted to avoid taking risks, enduring hard challenges, or facing uncomfortable situations. My intent was about nothing more than a comparison between two types of people: those who make things happen, and those who wait for things to happen.

After its initial release, the paper quickly circulated among military members, inspiring leadership sessions and ultimately reaching law enforcement and first responders. Remarkably, over a decade later, it remains a hot topic of discussion. This smashmouth approach to leadership has served people well over the years, with many asking me if I planned to expand the original thoughts set forth in 2012. After much deliberation, and based on the value the original text has provided for so many, I decided to accept the challenge. In this book, I will elaborate on the context behind each Silver Bullet via personal experiences over my thirty-three-year military career.

Critical to the success and resonation of these Silver Bullets, the input Janet brought to the balance of the original piece is invaluable but not accidental. As a military spouse, she has equally endured my hardships, struggles, successes, and evolution, often serving as my most trusted advisor. She was with me through my formative years, cutting my teeth as a special operator. She's been at my side through two decades of war, through physical and mental injuries, and through success and failure. She is my guiding light, my best friend, and the love of my life. To my Janet, thank you for being a kick-ass spouse, an honorable veteran, and a true patriot. You are a "meat eater" exemplified.

SILVER BULLETS FOR EFFECTIVE LEADERSHIP

In the spirit of full disclosure, I should acknowledge that I borrowed some of these concepts from already-known idioms or quotes and adapted them to align with the message I wanted to convey. We'll go into much more detail throughout the book, but for now, I've included a basic list of the twenty Silver Bullets below:

1. If you want to fly with the eagles, don't hang around with the turkeys.

2. The path to success is not easy, cheap, or quick. It will require getting up an hour earlier and going to bed an hour later.

3. The best way to stay in shape is to never get out of shape.

4. Amateurs train until they get it right; professionals train until they can't get it wrong.

5. Never pass up a great opportunity to shut the hell up if you have nothing productive to say.

6. Wherever you go, there you are—so make yourself useful.

7. Always leave the workplace better than how you found it.

8. The true aim of an education is not knowledge but action.

9. Never ask anyone to do anything that you are not willing to do yourself.

10. Where there is a choice to be made, there is a lesson to be learned.

11. Luck is when preparation and opportunity meet.

12. Image is a first impression; daily demeanor is a lasting impression.

13. Heroism is of the moment, but professionalism is a constant.

14. Loyalty is not mindless obedience.

15. Bad habits are like a comfortable bed: really easy to get into and really hard to get out of.

16. A life without humor is like a book without words.

17. Know the difference between "character" and "reputation."

18. A promise made is a promise kept.

19. Time management is a waste of time. Concentrate on "action" management instead.

20. Lead people with dignity and respect at all times.

As you load these twenty Silver Bullets into your thirty-round magazine, notice that there is still space for additional bullets. Take your successes and failures (referred to as powder for ammo) and write them down, along with the lessons learned (the shell casing). Pour the powder into the shell casing, place an "armor-piercing silver tip" on it, and load it into your magazine for future battles. Leadership is not an easy task, and most of the time, it will be an uphill fight. Regardless of the complexity of the battle, you must always be prepared to face the enemy and ensure your teammates are ready to cover your left, right, and rear flanks. Victory is a team endeavor. It is what we do; it is our way of life. We know no other way.

—*Your Carnivore Chief,*
~CZ

ALL HANDS... Humans vs. Hardware

• MDG IS THE MXG OF OUR HUMAN WEAPON SYSTEMS

– 20 Silver Bullets

1- EAGLES

2- OMELETTE

3- PATH TO

4- OVER REWARD

5- NEVER ASK...

6. BEST WAY TO ... SHARE

7- ACCEPT SET BACKS... LL

8- AIM OF ED.

9- OPP. TO SHUT UP

10- RESPECT EARNED

11- NOTHING EITHER GOOD OR BAD...

12- O IN COMMAND, N IN CHARGE

13- WHEREVER YOU GO, THERE YOU ARE.. SO MAKE YOURSELF USEFUL -

14- IMAGE IS 1ST IMP. CONDUCT IS LASTING -

This notecard shows an early iteration of the twenty silver bullets before I drafted the paper that garnered attention for my still-developing philosophy.

15- ALWAYS LEAVE IT BETTER THAN HOW YOU FOUND IT

16 - TELL LOVED ONES —

17- NO LUCK... #80

18- CHOICE, LESSON

19 - LETTER OR SPIRIT?

20. DON'T TRY... JUST BE

GROUP —

21 - BAD HABITS -

(*) ADD COMBAT TRANSLATION

ENTER THE CARNIVORE

Experience is an author's most valuable asset; experience is the thing that puts the muscle and the breath and the warm blood into the book he writes.
—Mark Twain

This is a book based on experience, not theory.

For as long as I can remember, I longed to be a man of action. I grew up in a small, rural town called Guánica in Puerto Rico, with limited means and possessions. As a young boy, I had an unlimited imagination and plenty of energy, and due to a rather precocious nature, my mother nicknamed me *espíritu adelantáo*: "advanced spirit." I attempted roller-skating at the age of two. By age three, I grew curious about underwater activities, and by five, gravity sports—specifically BMX bicycling. At seven, I took an interest in Kung Fu, and started jumping off of bridges into rivers. And by eleven, I was a damn good breakdancer.

I couldn't sit still. I was every mother's nightmare. And on top of all that, I was eccentric. I wore a webbed military belt to hold up my trousers, sometimes with a canteen attached to it. I often wore a cowboy hat, and I sported a Popeye pipe. By today's standards, I would've been heavily medicated, and likely shamed on social media.

All the activities above clearly cost money, something we didn't have much of, but the kids in my neighborhood always found a way to share, learn, and put into practice our ambitions. It was my first taste of teamwork, building alliances to achieve our common goals. We acted things out. We had a strong "let's do it" attitude, and while things didn't always work out as planned, at least we tried—and we always learned from it.

Some would believe that growing up in low-class neighborhoods would likely result in the following: permanent residency in a ghetto, a lack of education, being undercompensated for average work, and maybe even in prison due to poor choices and bad relationships. But as far back as I can remember, I dreamed of a better outcome, utilizing my imagination and aspirations as a wrecking ball to bring down the self-imposed barriers of my surroundings. While many choose to play the cards they are dealt, I chose to fold and reshuffle the deck in a quest for self-improvement and prosperity. I always believed in the possibility of a better hand and the value of gaining experience by consistently learning from my game strategy and failures. I chose to take charge of my actions, and focus on breaking away from the expectations or perceptions of others based on my environment. My shoulders were smooth and formed, absent of chips.

A vision without action is nothing more than an aspiration, no more than a wish or a dream. This book is about transforming vision into action via self-awareness, ownership, and control. I recall reading a cheesy motivational poster once that said, "Some dream of worthy accomplishments, while others wake up and realize them." I always ridiculed those posters. I figured that if that is what it took to motivate you, then you were unlikely to accomplish anything. But then I started thinking about the message, and it began to spark new thoughts and ideas, breaking my misperceptions and personal bias. I asked myself, what if I were to start writing down these random thoughts and then actualized and tested the intent? What if I were to start relating these thoughts to my passions? What if I could create vignettes to help others achieve success? And in 2005, that's exactly what I did. As I headed for the shooting range one day at Fort Bragg in North Carolina, I started penning down some thoughts on shooting and the discipline it takes to hit the target.

Here's what I wrote in my Moleskine notebook that day:

> *Like an expert marksman, you must know what you are aiming for. To have a clear vision equals keeping your target sight clear while eliminating the noise of your surroundings to properly focus and engage the target. The action that follows a clear sight picture is then squeezing, not pulling, the trigger to keep the weapon steady and the crosshairs trained on the intended impact area. The result is knowing whether you hit or missed the target by still looking through the sights, visualizing the impact of the bullet, and ensuring the target was properly engaged and down. Becoming an expert marksman takes practice, trial and error, and experience. So does becoming a leader. Leaders are not born; they are forged via personal courage, professionalism, and credibility.*

This was the original idea I used when I created the Silver Bullet paper seven years later, and the other four volumes that followed.

From that moment on, I thought of all the things I was passionate about and began writing passages in my Moleskine notebooks for the purpose of sharing my personal experiences with my subordinates. If I read a quote that resonated, I matched a personal experience to further explain it. I also got into the habit of visualizing the narrative and finding the best way to convey these ideas to my intended audiences via presentations and short papers. My notebooks also provided me an opportunity to purge frustration, capture good ideas, and analyze the thoughts and actions of others, enhancing my mental well-being. To this day, I collect my thoughts in the same fashion, and I continue to use these narratives for the personalization of speeches, for original storytelling, and to be genuine in my approach to communication.

These notebooks have served me well over the years, from my formative years as a special operator, to my appointment as the highest enlisted member of the entire US Department of Defense (DOD) as Senior Enlisted Advisor to the Chairman (SEAC) of the Joint Chiefs of Staff. Their impact to my self-awareness provided me an unfiltered inner perspective and an avenue to help others grow via relativity, recency, and reality. The adjustments I have been able to make in life have been driven by the lessons learned in this exciting and fearless method of accounting for my thoughts and actions. I used the notebooks all the way up until my last day in the military, serving at the Pentagon during extremely difficult times in recent American history, and I use them still to this day.

Regarding self-imposed limitations and freeing my mind from them, the experiential lessons I learned from my parents, having limited resources, exposed my sisters and me to an unsheltered world full of judgment, bias, skewed expectations, and lack of confidence. We were toughened up from an early age. We learned to deal with adversity and to value what little we had. While some may allow that environment to chart their path in life, I chose to pursue something better. What if I could defy the odds? What if I could make a difference in the lives of others? What if I could control the outcomes in my life? Enter the *Carnivore Leadership* mindset.

The original concept materialized during my time as a PJ in my first Joint Special Operations Command's (JSOC) National Mission Alert with a SEAL Team in Virginia Beach. This group of warriors are the few reserved for the most sensitive and critical missions, and we were ever ready to do whatever the nation needed from us. According to my boat crew leader, Jim Hintzke, we were classified into two groups there: Carnivores (meat eaters) or Herbivores (grass eaters).

Carnivores were loyal, dependable, lethal, and disciplined. Conversely, Herbivores were unreliable, lazy, and sloppy; they impeded operational progress. Herbivores were the whiners who expected more, in spite of their mediocre actions. The terms stuck. It was clear that there was only room for Carnivores. Herbivores inevitably proved themselves unworthy of our critical mission, and seldom stuck around.

After nearly a decade operating in such an uncompromising environment, the world became the battleground that helped me prove the concept, validating its relevance in cultures outside of the JSOC community. Carnivore leadership

THE VELOCIRAPTOR

When the time came to create my company Carnivore Concepts, I chose the velociraptor to represent the carnivore mindset for four reasons:

1. Its ferocious nature and focus to get its prey at any cost (determination).
2. Its intellect as one of the smartest predators of the prehistoric era.
3. Its affinity for teamwork to defeat bigger predators.
4. Its physical ability, speed, and strength for such a small predator, often besting larger opponents. The velociraptor best encapsulates the spirit of the meat-eater metaphor by being decisive, courageous, calculated, aggressive, and lethal.

is a method of self-reflection, maximizing the lessons we learn from our surroundings and extracting real-life examples for self-growth and the growth of our subordinates. Due to its positive effects in that highly selective community of special operators, I wanted to share it with my troops during my first assignment as a Command Senior Enlisted Leader. Little did I know then of the lasting effects this concept would have in the lives of many of our nation's warriors, first responders, and law enforcement personnel. To my amazement, it has even reached corporate America.

Carnivore Leadership encapsules the power to take control of your life through a journey sparked by learning, humble beginnings, and taking action. The content in this book is based on over three decades of military service to our nation as a special operator and culminating in service as SEAC during the most trying times in recent history. The odds were against me, truly a one-in-a-million chance,* but I figured out a way to beat the odds. I've grown accustomed to pushing past comfort zones. I've continued to reassess my actions, being critical of myself, valuing input from others, and continuing to learn. It helped me rise to the top in the DOD, and now I would like to share these thoughts with you.

As you read through the chapters, you will see connectivity, sequence, and relationship from one Silver Bullet to the other. This was not the intent when I wrote the original paper; it just coincidentally fell into place in rational order. Throughout the book are a few common themes like habits, ownership, courage, humility, bias for action, and growth. Over the past decade, I have been connecting the dots between these Silver Bullets to help others improve their leadership techniques via self-awareness and accountability. The results have been phenomenal in motivating some, helping others find their purpose, and even preventing suicide via the realization of self-worth. I am sure you will find value in applying these concepts in your daily activities, professional aspirations, and growth of your personnel.

Be aggressive, be factual, be humble, and be worthy of your people's time and care. Be a Carnivore!

---

* Only one service member gets to hold the SEAC position every four years, and only seventeen people out of 2.4 million can compete for the position, all of whom are in the top 1 percent of the Department of Defense enlisted force. Only one can reach the next level, hence 1 percent of 1 percent (0.0001). For further context, see the following link: https://www.jcs.mil/About/The-Joint-Staff/Senior-Enlisted-Advisor-to-the-Chairman/.

“

SILVER BULLET # 1

If you want to fly with the eagles, don't hang around with the turkeys.

It was a hot summer morning in San Antonio, Texas, when I reported to Lackland Air Force Base for my Pararescue Physical Ability and Stamina Test (PAST). The running track was littered with hopefuls, ready to put their mettle to the test. As I looked around, I wondered which of these men would be successful—myself included. This was the hardest training pipeline in the US military, and I did not have a full grasp on what was to come. The test would entail calisthenics in the form of push-ups, sit-ups, and pull-ups; a three-mile run at less than seven minutes per mile; and a 1,500-meter swim. I was stretching for the run when Staff Sergeant Terry Ness approached the group with a clipboard in his hands.

He began calling names in alphabetical order, dividing the candidates into groups. He then provided instructions on the sequence of events, followed by the standards of performance. As I mentally prepared to give my best physical performance, he uttered the following words: “Take a look around, ladies. This may be the last time you see some of these faces. This duty is not for everyone, and some of you came here under false hopes. Only the strong will remain standing." While I do not recall everything he said that day, those are the words that stuck in my head. They were a metaphorical slap in the face that woke me up to the reality of the expectations from this duty.

Terry Ness was a fit, small-statured man standing at about five-foot-six, and 150 pounds of solid muscle. He had battlefield credibility from the first Gulf War and was in good standing with the Air Force's Combat Control community. The man did not smile. He didn't show much emotion at all, in fact. But it was clear he meant every word he spoke. The scene was set, and it was time to perform, to prove to this man and the other instructor that we were worthy of the company.

The first event was the calisthenics. The majority did well, with only a few not meeting minimum standards. After a short break, the three-mile run commenced, and we lost a few more there. After the next break leading to the final event (swimming), the group was much smaller: if memory serves me correctly, we lost 30 to 40 percent of the original pool of candidates.

After I completed all phases of the test and earned a spot on my Pararescue and Combat Control selection course, I noticed a change within. I developed a hunger to experience the uncertainty and to further test myself. I also gained an appreciation for those willing to endure and persevere under such painful conditions, willing to sacrifice comfort to find purpose.

During the first twelve weeks, many more succumbed to the rigors and demands of the program. My circle of friends became smaller, not by choice but by attrition. I saw many good men fall by the wayside, and I gained friendships and a brotherhood that remains to this today. Of all the friends I made during the selection course, there was a core group of five of us, best friends that included me, Judd Woehrle, Bob Simmons, Joe Conroy, and my bunkmate, J.J. Baker—my "comic relief" sidekick.

J.J. was from New York and was very easy to like. He had previous experience in the program, which made him a valuable resource. He also had one of the greatest senses of humor I had ever encountered. He had an ability to break the tension in the most stressful of times. Together, we were a team in charge of keeping the humor rolling throughout the greatest crucible of our lives; we felt we had a duty to help our teammates, as they helped us via other means, motivating each other to carry on becoming Pararescuemen and Combat Controllers.

As a solid and committed instructor, Terry Ness left a positive impression on me. He was the type of person I wanted to become, the first "influencer" in my quest to become a Pararescueman.

Influencers today are a dime a dozen, and some make millions based on their online following. Back in my youth, "influencers" were the company you kept, the people closest to you. When I was a kid, my parents were concerned about the company I kept. They required my sisters and me to be around people that were good-natured and familiar, and they frowned upon association with the neighborhood's "bad seeds." The first question they would ask whenever I left the house was "Who are you going out with?" Even though they were fully aware of my daredevil tendencies, the company I kept was the deciding factor in whether I had permission to participate.

I had the freedom to ride my bike, go to the beach, engage in sports, and even head into town—if I was with the right crowd.

Charging down steep hills on my Big Wheel pretending to be Evel Knievel, and jumping off twelve-foot rooftops pretending to be Steve Austin, no problem. Being at the brink of shallow-water blackout in the ocean, competing with my cousins on who could stay underwater the longest, sure. But not being around responsible and dependable people? That was an absolute no-go. It was one of the earliest examples I can remember of the power of trust.

Coupled with trust, that freedom taught me that influence and interaction are a training ground that eventually molds us into our future selves, the stage for the best educational experience of our existence. This self-actualization, discovery, and validation not only gave me confidence in my abilities, but it also shaped me into a critical thinker and risk analyzer, a student of my surroundings. As I grew older, I started analyzing the "why" of many things, including the restrictions and concerns my parents had diligently adhered to over the years regarding the influencers in my life. I began paying more attention to the character of the people rather than their popularity and social standing. I gauged the level of relationship I would have with any given person based on their values and drive. Not having a good gut feeling about people's intentions became the warning light on my dashboard of influence. Looking back, it doesn't surprise me that the times I didn't listen to my parents, I ended up in bad situations with regretful outcomes—and the same is true for when I disregarded my own gut feelings.

In my teens, my compliance with this character gauge would come and go, but that was part of growing up and having fun. It wasn't until my enrollment at a Catholic high school that I took this approach seriously. "If you want to fly with the eagles, don't hang around with the turkeys." The first time I heard this was during an admission briefing with Father Frank Wiesel, the principal of Kolbe Cathedral High School. In the process of setting the conditions for my tuition assistance, expected grade point average, and follow-on plans, he said that the company we kept would eventually shape us as humans and that we would become a product of our environment. Based on the way I had grown up, this resonated with me.

After receiving that guidance from Father Wiesel, excuses for behavior became scarce, and ownership of actions became more commonplace. As students, we were accountable for our schoolwork, our behavior, our actions, and our shortcomings by regularly reporting to Father Wiesel. While of course we regressed from time to time—we were ignorant teenagers, after all—the frequent touchpoints with our principal served as a vector check that often steered us in the direction of value, professionalism, and honesty. Those lessons and advice from someone we respected and admired served as a moral compass to get us on track. Father Wiesel was the first "eagle" I ever followed. In retrospect, it wasn't so much the quote but rather the expectations Father Wiesel set forth that made the difference. I learned the value of influence and discipline, something that eventually pointed me in the direction of military service.

Upon enlisting in the United States Air Force at the age of nineteen, the rules, ethos, and expectations of military service served as a quality control mechanism for relationships. The military's strict standards of behavior, appearance, and adherence to orders made it easier to find the company of eagles, primarily because the military is not a conducive environment for the behavior of turkeys. If a "turkey" didn't live up to the standards of military service, Thanksgiving came early and his lifespan was short. This became clear when I assessed to become a Pararescueman (PJ), when I realized the value of the company you keep is an equalizer for survival. To be a member of a tribe in which physical and mental pain is a rite of passage, sacrifice and hard work were nonnegotiable. We had to prove ourselves worthy to be among the select few who could step out of the realm of comfort and into the great unknown.

I entered the arduous Pararescue training pipeline in early 1993 after serving previously as an administrator, specifically an Air Force Traffic Management Office Airman. I was the guy that helped military people move from location to location, a move manager—basically a travel agent, which was a gross mismatch for my personality. I didn't know much about Pararescue prior to taking the initial test for entry, the one that required calisthenics, swimming, and running. It didn't take long to realize that it would be the hardest mental and physical test of my life, as I saw many of my peers fail and quit in the process.

When my class started after taking the PAST test, we had 113 candidates beginning the initial twelve-week program. By week five, we were at about half of that, and by the end of the assessment and selection, there were only twelve of us left standing, more than a 90 percent attrition rate. That small group exposed me to a more precise definition of what an "eagle" was: a person with motivation, drive, intellect, and a servant spirit—a person who is willing to sacrifice all to give someone else a second chance at life. Our motto was "These things we do, that others may live," and we truly lived by it. Those words not only defined our purpose but also validated the employment of our abilities in an arena where many fail.

After becoming a PJ, I have had the honor of meeting many eagles (too many to mention in this book), some who have become lifelong friends. There is a hierarchy of eagles in my life, the main ones being my mother, Vilma, and my wife, Janet—the two most caring, funny, and honest people in the whole world. Secondly, while many have invested in my quest for leadership development, I must name four eagles who made a significant difference in my life: Wayne Fisk, Bob Gaylor, Jim Binnicker, and Jim Slife. I call these gentlemen my Mount Rushmore of leadership. Their insights, lessons, advice, friendship, and counsel have helped shape me into the best version of myself, as both a warrior and a man. And third are those who helped shape the warrior within me, from PJs Gary Lewry and Jim Rothermel, to Combat Controllers (CCTs) Mike Lamonica and Vinnie Venturella, to name a few. Once you truly identify the direction you want to go in life, these entities will appear along the way to help you carry the load, as we cannot accomplish anything worthy in this life on our own.

The essence of this Silver Bullet is to be cognizant of your relationships, your surroundings, and the climate and accountability of your organization. Effective leaders associate with people who help them improve the organization and themselves, often in the form of challenges that force us outside of the routine and mundane. These role models—the eagles—are deliberate in the development of others to continue a cycle of excellence. They are humble enough to accept criticism and feedback, and they are often quiet professionals who let their actions speak for them. They are the ones who create a strong following due to their credibility. Eagles are a necessary component in any organization that wants to maintain a competitive edge. Look around you and take notice of who the eagles are and who the turkeys are, as these two eventually morph into the Carnivores and Herbivores in your life.

SILVER BULLET #2

The path to success is not easy, cheap, or quick. It will require getting up an hour earlier and going to bed an hour later.

A common saying rooted in blues and Jamaican culture says, "Everybody wants to go to heaven, but nobody wants to die." People often expect high rewards for minimal work. They harbor a sense of entitlement, thinking that if they merely show up, they deserve something in return. But this thinking is flawed.

The second Silver Bullet is often taken out of context, mistaken as an afflictive approach to success. "The path to success is not easy, cheap, or quick. It will require getting up an hour earlier and going to bed an hour later." I once wrote it as a social media post, and people blasted the poor practice of working yourself to death. They insisted it promoted a stressful work environment, a lack of sleep, and so on. Enter the grass eater—the Herbivore—always searching for ways to make things easy and shirk the responsibility of hard work. To clear it up for the naysayers, I'm simply saying that if you want to be successful, you must work harder. You must do more than the minimum.

Let me take you back to 2005, the year I left JSOC and reported for duty at the PJ School in Albuquerque, New Mexico. Upon checking in with my unit, I saw many familiar faces, even some that had entered the training pipeline with me in 1993. During a conversation with one of my teammates, he remarked that I was "lucky to have a career experience unlike others."

My response came quickly and from the gut. "It has nothing to do with luck," I told him. "I just decided to stay on the path of my goals. I refused to deviate from the course." I imagine my reply stung a bit, mainly due to the indecisiveness of the teammate who had made the comment. You see, he wasn't sure if he wanted to remain a PJ. He wondered if he should instead attend medical school, go to law school, or become something else entirely. The difference between him and me was that I had a strong sense of direction—a clear focus on my azimuth. I could picture my next steps. For him, it was difficult to envision a journey, especially while allowing every exit and detour to distract him along the way.

To achieve success, we must be deliberate in our approach. It begins with deciding on a destination, a route of march, a desired end point, all with a clear and attainable goal. Then we must analyze our capabilities and limitations, real and perceived, prior to embarking on our journey. Subsequently, we must remain flexible and ready to deal with obstacles in the way of achievement. We must remain committed to our goal, even in the face of hardship. Commitment is critical; accepting the requisite sacrifices is crucial in gaining an edge over the average. This means taking that extra step, even when we're tired. It means maintaining optimism, preparing and adjusting in real time, and consistently gauging progress with diligent patience along the way.

It takes discipline, commitment, and patience to do this. A lack of these attributes is the antagonist of achievement. In a world that craves immediate results, a leader must have the patience to see things play out and deal with contingencies. Commitment provides a leader with the belief in the actions necessary to accomplish a feat. Patience helps you think about, reflect upon, and study the many possibilities and opportunities of the moment. A combination of commitment and patience will help you deal with adversity, failure, rejection, setbacks, and criticism. And it is discipline that will keep you moving in the direction of success. This trinity of discipline, commitment, and patience is the foundation of decisive individuals, whereas the indecisive ones often lack patience, which leads to a lack of commitment and an erosion of self-discipline.

The path to achieve my goals began in 1993, when I committed my life to Pararescue. It was my "a-ha" moment, the realization that I had a purpose in life. The meaning in my actions became clear and tangible. Sacrifice became a habit; I accepted it and expected it with every move I made because the challenges were never easy. The more I lived this way, the better my life became. I became a better person. I was energized and driven. I was committed. I was all in, never afraid of failure, and fully aware of my surroundings and my relationships.

The setbacks were ever present, but I remained patient and open-minded so I could properly analyze every situation and strive for a better outcome. I also remained committed to my profession, unwavering in my mission and loyalty to the team.

These disciplined habits also helped curb my personal biases and improve my understanding of others. But the most valuable outcome was an ability to shape organizational climate, culture, environment, and even people.

Outside influences will attempt to stall your progress, mainly out of envy. You have choices when considering their feedback. If it is of value, accept it. If it is constructive, utilize it. If it is unsubstantiated, discard it. And if it comes from someone who has never experienced what you are about to embark upon, ignore it. These choices will be part of your analytical thinking process as you weigh your options. I must also point out that there is value in the negativity of others, especially when they tell you that a feat is impossible. In my case, the naysayers became tinder for the fire in my gut, fueling my desire for success. There is nothing more satisfying as a leader than to accomplish goals that people deem unattainable. To do so requires hard work, time, and vision.

The last four of my thirty-three years in the military were by far the most challenging. The political environment in Washington, DC, along with the social unrest plaguing the country at the time, the COVID-19 pandemic, the withdrawal from Afghanistan, and the conflict in Ukraine were some of the key issues I dealt with as a senior leader in the DOD. The amount of critical advice to senior leaders both in the military and in government, the consistent fight against polarizing narratives, and the exhausting endeavor of communicating facts to a force of 2.4 million people really took a toll on me. In addition to all of the above, I was struggling with both physical and mental issues residual from twenty years in combat, both as a warrior and as a leader. Upon culminating my tour of duty as the SEAC, Janet asked me, "Was the duty everything you thought it would be?"

"It was everything I thought I could make of it." I replied instinctively.

I had come into the position knowing I needed to make some changes to validate the purpose and value of duty as the SEAC. It was a new position in the DOD at the time, and some leaders questioned its value—including former chairmen of the Joint Chiefs of Staff (CJCS) and a group of four-star generals in very prominent positions. During my interview with General Mark A. Milley, the first thing he said was, "I have been advised by many not to fill this position. They see it as a waste of time, and more trouble than it's worth. Tell me, why should I select a SEAC?"

My first thoughts were *Why the hell am I here?* and *Is this a waste of time for the both of us?* But my self-awareness kicked in and countered with *What are the gaps that created that perception, and what are General Milley's needs when it comes to a vision and direction for the DOD?*

"If you were to fill the position, what is your expected return on this investment?" I asked. It was at that moment that we began exploring possibilities, figuring out what "right" would look like for our tenure and beyond. And when I was announced as General Milley's selection, I immediately went to work on my research and plan for the way ahead.

Upon arriving at the Pentagon, I came to discover that many in the CJCS staff did not value the position and wished to eliminate it. The previous SEAC's resources had been divided among the directorates, and the office was left minimally manned. Additionally, everyone was quick to remind me that the position was "only temporary" and that they were not sure if the next CJCS would retain it. This led to a daily struggle to justify the resources needed to make a difference.

My task from day one was to validate the value of this critical leadership position, even against the advice of high-ranking officers and prominent figures such as former CJCS and Secretary of State Colin Powell, who stated publicly that he "did not see a need for the position." The "easy button" would've been for me to say screw it and just coast along collecting pay, playing it safe while traveling, handing out challenge coins, and eating chicken dinners. It seemed everyone was willing to light the path to failure and omission, but no one wanted to explore the way to success. It was not the way I was accustomed to doing things.

My other option was to work hard—to justify, solidify, and bring credibility to the position. This was the way of the Carnivore. To those who insisted that the position wasn't worth it, I decided, "Bring it on. Challenge accepted." Many made the case to give up, to throw in the towel. What they didn't realize was that I was accustomed to taking hits. Just like boxing, I knew when to swing, when to guard, and most importantly, when to take the eight-count to regroup.

So how do you swim against such a powerful tide of disapproval and lack of confidence? There is only one way, and that is to prove the opposite. Many would walk away from such a challenge, but not a meat eater—not a Carnivore. In my life, there have been many situations in which others tried to tell me something couldn't be done, and I always took the approach to do one thing: to show them it *could* be done.

To show them, I took charge of my duty. I didn't leave it to chance or luck. I took a deliberate approach to shaping the role and responsibility of the position, based on habits built through many crucibles in life to achieve the expected outcomes of the CJCS. Step one was to instill belief in the value of the SEAC. Step two was to align with the empowerment and expected actions of the position. And step three was to provide continuous results and accountability. After receiving initial guidance from the CJCS, I reflected on the lessons I had learned, and I developed a plan for action. This habit of operationalizing and turning vision into action had begun early on, long before my military service. Through self-reflection and accountability, I had become a student of my surroundings, even in my early years living life to the fullest on the island of Puerto Rico, and I used it in my quest for success as the SEAC.

Getting up an hour earlier and going to bed an hour later, literally and figuratively, allowed me to endure two years of pain, anguish, hardship, and sacrifice during the most grueling crucible of my life: becoming a Pararescueman. It also helped me prove the naysayers wrong when I fulfilled the duty of being the SEAC. As I've matured on my journey, those habits have transcended into my personal life—in my marriage, my interpersonal relationships, various projects I take on, and even in writing this book. The acceptance of sacrifice will help you kill procrastination, doubt, and fear. Your discipline will help you develop into a living example, a role model. Do not take shortcuts. Dare to tackle the impossible. Give it all a chance, knowing you are willing and able to put in the extra work required of excellence.

SILVER BULLET #3

The best way to stay in shape is to never get out of shape.

When you first meet someone, what grabs your attention? Is it their charm, their eloquence, their intellect, their appearance? It may be a combination of those qualities, where one strength makes up for the lack of another. But even when a strength makes up for another, there is usually a discriminator that takes away from the true value of a person. Too harsh, too clumsy, too dumb, or too sloppy creates a hole hard to climb out of and tarnishes the perception of one's qualities.

In the special operations community, image and fitness are prominent discriminators, often seen as the vessel of a warrior. But physical strength and appearance are merely the shell of a warrior. The mental health of these highly trained professionals is equally as important. If you're physically out of shape, there's a good chance you'll be unable to perform or endure. On the mental side, if your character is flawed and your motivation is lacking, you're likely to make stupid decisions or fail to perform, tarnishing the reputation of the organization. The lethality and effectiveness of a warrior hinges upon a combination of mental and physical prowess.

For the warrior class, not being in shape is an indicator of poor self-discipline and a killer of credibility. The elements of performance and reliability are nonnegotiable for everyone on the team, including support personnel. That culture, coupled with the responsibility of a critical and uncertain mission, created some of the best leaders I have had the honor to serve with. For all assigned, male or female, operator or support, the expectation is the same: do your job. To further elaborate, "do your job" means anywhere, anytime, under any circumstances. Special ops warriors are trained and conditioned to build strong bodies and strong minds.

This expectation is not exclusive to special operations personnel; it applies to all who serve in the military. A military member must look the part, act the part, and be the part. Doing so allows the public to have confidence in their defenders of the Constitution. Their image and comportment are critical to the reputation of the institution, and their availability and employment are byproducts of the sacrifices they make to meet the demands of service. A healthy body and mind are a requirement for military service, regardless of occupation or standing. And even though less than 15 percent of servicemembers are expected to see combat, the majority will have to deploy to all sorts of environments. The promotion of health in military service is primarily to ensure the deployability of the individual. Paraphrasing the words of former Secretary of Defense James Mattis, there is no room for fatties, and if you are not worldwide deployable, we don't want you.

The importance of good physical and mental fitness cannot be understated, even in everyday life. Most recently, during the

COVID-19 pandemic, military forces maintained their readiness and world-wide deployment ability due to strict regimens and standards associated with physical fitness and mental resilience. The military, in turn, was able to provide support to civil authorities throughout the entire period of emergency, sending a resounding message to our enemies that, regardless of the situation, our military is ready to respond. Because of its limits on age and time in service, the military has a requirement for generational commitment to service in the armed forces. The same can be said about first responders and other professions that require both brain and brawn. This is becoming more problematic for Americans as our youth becomes more sedentary and less available for service.

As we look at society today, obesity and poor health are key factors in preventing 76 percent of our youth between eighteen and twenty-four years of age to serve our nation as first responders or military members. This is a national issue for America but not a new one. We faced the same problem at the beginning of the Korean War, which later prompted President Kennedy to begin a national program for the fitness of our youth. In a 1960 article published in *Sports Illustrated*, here's what then-president-elect John F. Kennedy wrote:

> But the harsh fact of the matter is that there is also an increasingly large number of young Americans who are neglecting their bodies—whose physical fitness is not what it should be—who are getting soft. And such softness on the part of individual citizens can help strip or destroy the vitality of a nation.

> For the physical vigor of our citizens is one of America's most precious resources. If we waste and neglect this resource, if we allow it to dwindle and grow soft then we will destroy much of our ability to meet the great and vital challenges which confront our people. We will be unable to realize our full potential as a nation.*

The same stands true today, but there has been a shift in the mindset, where our society has accepted obesity as a right or even a badge of courage instead of a disease, and our youth are paying the price. The promotion of plus-sized clothing and models, and an insistence that "big is beautiful" is creating a "plus-sized" problem that is anything but beautiful. Obesity is a disease, it costs taxpayers billions of dollars in healthcare every year, and it is placing our national security in jeopardy by making our youth a generation of spectators. The health of American people is critical to our prosperity, but it is an individual responsibility and a duty of parents to coach their children to be healthy.

To live a healthy life, one must create a pattern of proper diet and fitness to prevent disease and to be mentally ready to deal with adversity. Change is possible. We do it every week in our basic military training institutions. In the military, the standards and rules are set; accountability and expectations are clear. The strict nature of this discipline makes it easy for most to comply. And those who do not comply get accounted for and disciplined. We speak of discipline in the sense of correction

* President-Elect John F. Kennedy, "The Soft American," *Sports Illustrated*, December 26, 1960.

and not punishment. The punishment comes if you are a repeat offender. One thing I love about the military approach to correction is its bluntness and colorful nature. I, as well as many other master chiefs and sergeants major, employ such bluntness to build up, not to break down. We use it to get the culprit's undivided attention.

In my original paper about the Silver Bullets, I described the appearance of an out-of-shape military member in uniform as looking like "a marshmallow wrapped in dental floss." This was meant to be provocative, a slap back to reality. There is no room for coddling in battle, or in preparation to do battle, hence our blunt approach. You either get with the program, or find another place to exist. And once you get in shape, it is important to stay in shape.

New Year's resolutions and other temporary approaches to fitness are not the answer. Fitness brand Peloton saw a substantial spike in sales and membership during the pandemic, reaching a "peak intraday share price of $167" in December 2020—but it didn't last.* While much of the world was on lockdown, spending more time at home and less time in gyms or outdoors, people looked to Peloton as a solution for at-home fitness, but later sales dips indicated it was more of a novelty than an overall shift toward healthy habits. Habits must be consistent and sacred, a contract for life. A parent that maintains healthy habits serves as an example. A leader that does this sets expectations for subordinates. And individuals that

* Gabriel Fonrouge, "Inside Peloton's Rapid Rise and Bitter Fall—and Its Attempt at a Comeback," CNBC, February 19, 2023, https://www.cnbc.com/2023/02/19/peloton-rise-fall-attempted-comeback.html.

do this are simply going to be the best versions of themselves, living healthy and joyous lives.

When we achieve peak fitness, it is our personal responsibility to maintain it. A setback can create a biological backlog on the wellness of the individual. We have all experienced this at some point in our lives. A fitness setback can also be detrimental to your credibility. To motivate my troops while serving in the military, I always chose to get my hands dirty and accept my troops' challenges without reservation. I've been tazed and pepper-sprayed by cops and bit by a military working dog. I've participated in a marksmanship shooting challenge, accepted multiple physical fitness challenges, dug ditches with our civil engineers, and even helped fix a broken sewage line after noticing our troops working on it on the side of the road.

Unfortunately, though, not all leaders are created equally. I've witnessed ill-prepared and lazy leaders who pass on those opportunities simply because they had not been keeping up with their fitness. In one particular case, an enlisted leader refused to partake in a group physical training (PT) session because his PT test was in a few days, and he wanted to save himself from injury. The look on the faces of his troops spoke a thousand words of disappointment, as their leader stood on the sidelines in a pressed uniform watching the rest of us sweat it out in the mud. Pathetic, to say the least.

In leadership, we do not have the luxury to pick and choose which standards to exemplify. All this man had to do was meet the expectations of his people by accepting the challenge. His fear of failure proved counterproductive. Instead of saving face, he lost credibility. His lack of commitment and dedication to a standard eroded the trust and confidence of his followers and marginalized the validity of the military requirement of physical readiness. To prevent this from happening in any organization, discipline, accountability, and consistency in execution must be ever present. Physical health is a part of it, and a critical one indeed, but also keep the mental aspect at the forefront. In the end, be the example. Act the part, look the part, and be the part. Make health and fitness a habit. Promote it via your daily actions.

SILVER BULLET #4

Amateurs train until they get it right; professionals train until they can't get it wrong.

A professional is someone who adheres to both the technical and ethical standards of a profession. Can a person be a true professional if they adhere to one but not the other—if they possess technical prowess but not ethical, or vice versa? In my experience, the answer is no. The best leaders I've known have been those who possess both trade credibility and solid character. They are the "gurus" of their profession, promoting both ethical behavior and technical proficiency. Technical proficiency leads to credibility and reliability, and high ethical standards lead to honorable character and exemplary behavior.

A professional is more than a "box checker." He or she does not strive for only the bare minimum, or embellish his or her curriculum vitae. Many disappointed employers struggle with this "not as advertised" dilemma. People often oversell themselves. They deliver a false first impression just to get their foot in the door. Imagine the disappointment of welcoming an employee who is expected to walk on water, but after the honeymoon period wears off, they quickly sink to the bottom of a pool of lies. This con-artist approach is common, unfortunately, where the pen—or keyboard—is mightier than the individual's character, worth, and capabilities. They are simply amateurs pretending to be professionals.

A professional strives for perfection and muscle memory. This was ingrained in me in 1993 while attending the Pararescue and Combat Control selection course. Every training day was harsh, from early morning to late evenings. Rest was scarce and recovery was limited, but high performance was always expected. We began with an early morning run, followed by a grueling calisthenics session, then classes on dive physics and metrics, culminating with the dreaded and incredibly difficult water-based challenges. The only choice was to perform. There was no time to fake it.

At the end of the first twelve weeks, we had lost 90 percent of the class. That high attrition rate was based on the requirement to be both mentally and physically fit and meeting measurable standards with a pass-or-fail grade requirement both on the physical and intellectual fronts. For example, at the end of the course, each candidate had to perform a specific number of push-ups, pull-ups, and sit-ups in perfect form and within a certain time constraint. We had to run six miles at a pace of less than seven minutes per mile and complete a 3,000-meter fin swim in less than a minute per 50 meters. Those expectations forced each team member to train to achieve success with a no-fail mentality. The old saying "I can do that blindfolded" rang true for successful candidates, often because we had to perform in blacked-out rooms to mimic the darkest hours of night, in austere environments, or in the deep seas that often served as a rescue arena for operations. The habit of striving for perfection, inculcated early in our training, paved the way for technical proficiency and, in turn, professionalism. We eliminated the chance of being called amateurs, because we trained until we couldn't get it wrong.

What I learned in those early days transcended into my future career as a Tier 1 operator. Our method to strive for perfection was based on repetition, practice, and discovery—what some call "reps and sets." For example, when it came to my tactical equipment configuration and the contents of my rescue backpack, it took me at least seven training scenarios to get familiar with placement and access, and to set my standard. This "trial and error" approach allowed me to develop confidence in my equipment based on my ability to react quickly to contingencies based on familiarity. I could get to any of my equipment blindfolded . . . literally!

The benefit of this habit was not solely for the individual to achieve success; it was also to share lessons with the broader team across three services. The amazing part was that most of our teammates were doing the same thing, validating their capabilities and effectiveness. We were a master "think tank" of tactical development. Often, the practices and configurations we developed became the gold standard for many in the military outside of special ops. This type of behavior created a healthy peer pressure for improvement that, in turn, created our nation's most professional organization. To this day, I utilize this approach in everyday life.

In practice and application, this "reps and sets" mentality to achieve professional perfection can be applied to any segment of society. Sports teams do it. School debate teams do it. Contestants even do it in hot-dog-eating competitions. Why? Because they know the rules, the expectations, and the desired outcome—all of which serve as a map and compass on their path in the direction of success. And this is not limited to competition or combat. For instance, as I write my own speeches and practice my delivery, I make sure to apply the "reps and sets" process in drafting and finalizing, often with Janet as my best critic to make sure I don't get it wrong or waste anyone's time. Do it long enough, and it will become a hard habit to break.

I would even go a step further and apply the concept to relationship maintenance, referring in particular to honey-do lists. I have been on the losing end of this equation, where Janet sees the effort I put into work but not into my home chores. By virtue of experiencing over three decades alongside me, she knows what I am capable of. She knows I can make time for things that I am focused on. She knows that when I apply myself to something, I am likely to achieve success. And most importantly, she knows that if I care enough, I will be deliberate in the quest of mastering a task. That experience and awareness of my capabilities and drive is her measurement and accountability mechanism. If I fall short, she can shoot holes through any excuse I offer, just as easily as she can shoot a deer from 220 yards.

A consistent approach, without shortcuts, is the best way to develop the habit of seeking perfection. Patience in execution and acceptance of outcomes play into the value of your approach. Keep in mind that if you do not seek perfection, it will only create a shallow capability, one that often leads to failure. Train to the point of muscle memory. Do not oversell yourself if you haven't done the work. Be ready to execute at all times.

SILVER BULLET #5

Never pass up a great opportunity to shut the hell up if you have nothing productive to say.

One of the worst things about being in a key military leadership position is the number of daily briefings one must attend. While overcommunication and transparency are great for awareness, long-winded meetings are motivation's greatest foe. They are antithetical to the productive intent of sharing information and can create stress by stealing productivity time away from your people. I recall many times wishing for a firefight rather than enduring someone's mundane pontification on irrelevant topics.

While briefings and meetings are necessary to ensure mission, vision, expectations, and transparency for key stakeholders, they should not be a source of angst. The stress and anxiety of watching valuable time slip away are counterproductive to high-performing organizations. And the culprits of these problematic meetings are the people who love to hear themselves talk without having anything of substance to say.

Picking up where we left off in the previous chapter, the Silver Bullet on developing professional habits, the key to a productive meeting is to be well-versed on the topic and be prepared to add value if needed. Knowing your responsibilities and the variables affecting the expected outcome are a requirement if you are invited to the conversation. While not required to speak, if your topic of responsibility comes up and there are questions, you must be ready to deliver. But if there is no value to the soundwaves exiting your piehole, then it's best to exercise silence.

If you speak only when you can add value, you will develop a reputation for being a productive and considerate communicator, and others will pause and give you their full attention. On the other hand, if you're in the habit of flapping your soup-coolers for no good reason, with nothing of value to contribute to the conversation, people will start doodling, eye-rolling, or sighing. Next time you speak at a meeting, scan the room for the reaction of your peers. Pay attention, and if needed, start implementing changes in your style and preparation habits.

Next, we have those who attend meetings for other reasons, none of which adds any value. Some attend simply to have face-time with the boss. Others attend for the sole purpose of ass-kissing. Such people exemplify the definition of "mass" by merely "occupying space" in the boardroom, or being the "spring butt" that must have a stage to say something. A "spring butt" is that ass-kisser in class who seems to have all the answers and makes a habit of jumping out of his or her chair in an attempt to impress everyone. They often speak even if they are not adding value: the masters of the obvious, and the barnacles on the ass of progress.

To add value when communicating, one must be deliberate

in their delivery. I like to use the analogy of a bolt-action hunting rifle. Utilizing this "bolt-action" mentality, you first load the round. Then you chamber it by driving the bolt forward. And then you exercise discipline while squeezing the trigger, keeping a clear sight of the target. For the purposes of this analogy, "loading the round" means doing your research, validating assumptions, and gathering facts. "Chambering the round" means structuring the communication plan to ensure that your audience will understand your message. And "squeezing the trigger" means being brief and concise while sticking to the intended point of focus. Much like shooting, this approach will ensure the proper intended use of your weapon—in this case, your mouth—and it will also conserve ammo (your valued input) for when it is truly needed.

The opposite of this is when the speaker aimlessly sprays ammunition in the direction of what they believe is the target, hoping they hit something—known tactically as "spray and pray." This rapid firing without clear sight of a target is a waste of ammunition and a waste of the intended audience's time. You also run the risk of hitting unintended targets, metaphorically speaking, and damaging your credibility.

To avoid falling victim to this rapid-fire scenario, it's best before the meeting to take a knee, collect your thoughts, and think about what you want to say. Being ill-prepared often leads to this rapid firing. Being overly eager to impress leads to a waste of ammunition. Veering off topic and bringing up irrelevant agendas leads to empty weapons that should be reserved for some other fight. Don't be the "spray and pray" kind. To effectively deliver your intended message, be a sniper.

Long ago, I heard someone say that there's a reason we

have one mouth and two ears—and we should use them in proportion. Sometimes listening to the concerns, input, and agendas of others can help you prepare for the next round of communication. It can also facilitate a fruitful exchange with peers that have certain responsibilities outside of your own that may be related. It may help you craft more effective oral or written communications to further solidify your position on a given topic before delivery. But listening takes patience, and patience is a lost virtue in today's society. Set yourself apart from the pack by being a quiet professional, one who listens with intent, one who rationalizes the messaging, and one who delivers unbiased opinions and input. Develop a reputation for being the organizational communicator that hits the target every time: one shot, one kill.

This self-awareness and habit for preparation will present you as a calculated marksman aiming for the center mass of the target. The more often you hit the target, the faster you will earn credibility, and the more people will listen to what you have to say. This is how you add value to communication and, in turn, to the progress of the organization.

Remember, as the Silver Bullet states, "Never pass up a great opportunity to shut the hell up if you have nothing productive to say." Be purposeful, studied, and relevant to add value, not time, to the topic of discussion.

SILVER BULLET #6

Wherever you go, there you are—so make yourself useful.

In my three decades as a special operator and leader, I have encountered many people struggling to find their purpose in life. Some carry on, day by day, earning a paycheck but hating their jobs. Others struggle to stay on a path that will help them reach a desired destination. And some are just lost like last year's Easter eggs, indecisive in their purpose or goals. But the most desperate people I have encountered are those who are willing to sell their soul for an assignment or position while overselling their capabilities on paper and trampling over anyone who gets in their way.

Let's first talk about the "make yourself useful" part of this Silver Bullet. While learning from past successes can help us gain an advantage in competition, it can also create a false sense of trajectory toward our desired destination. For example, in the US Air Force, the most coveted position as an enlisted troop is the achievement of CMSAF (Chief Master Sergeant of the Air Force), the top dog in the arena for that service. In order to compete for that position, to even be considered, senior enlisted leaders need to fulfill certain progressive assignments with increased responsibilities. Then, after one fulfills those assignments required for eligibility, only a handful will get the opportunity to present their case to the hiring authority—in this case, the Chief of Staff of the Air Force, the highest-ranking general officer of that service.

Herein lies the problem. People tend to overglamorize themselves in order to impress. I equate this to the "successful first date" phenomenon, where, upon that first encounter, things seem nearly perfect and you return home thinking you found "the one." But then comes the discovery period, when you find out the true nature of a person, those little details concealed beneath the surface—the quirks that often become exhausting to conceal in the long term, the face you wake up to every morning in its natural state. You see, pretending can only take you as far as you can keep up the lie. Eventually, you'll slip and your true colors will surface, forcing the other party to make a decision to stay and tolerate the lemon they've been sold, or to break away from the relationship. And this goes beyond dating. For any employer out there, this is not a position they want to be in.

Many people believe that previous successes will perpetually aid their progression; they rest on their laurels. In the Air Force enlisted ranks, there are three tiers: airmen (most junior), noncommissioned officers (middle leaders, also known as NCOs), and senior noncommissioned officers (the top leaders, SNCOs). Via personal experience and by witnessing the careers of others, I can attest to the fact that success as an airman does not guarantee success as an NCO. Subsequently, success as an NCO does not guarantee success as a SNCO. But mediocrity in any tier will certainly guarantee failure at the next. The best remedy to this pitfall is to continuously reassess your capabilities, continuously learn and adapt, and continuously seek the advice of those you admire (your eagles) in order to avoid developing an inflated ego due to the successes of today.

The best way to make yourself useful and to mitigate this self-aggrandizing behavior is to continuously prove yourself via actions, while living up to the reputation cemented by those past successes. To be "as advertised" by the paper that sells you is to perform to that standard and to show consistent progression. The best way for anyone to portray themselves authentically is to let their actions do the talking. Your focus should be on nothing more than crushing every task you are given, innovating toward the evolution of the organization, taking calculated chances, and displaying ownership of your responsibilities every time.

So, what about the "wherever you go" part of this Silver Bullet? This refers to the dues you must pay to get to where you ultimately want to be. Regardless of trade or profession, there is often a crucible to prove your worth and loyalty to an organization, paved by sometimes undesirable and menially perceived positions not appealing to our self-proclaimed worth. A long time ago in my military career, I stopped worrying about the "next assignment." While locations and desired organizations mattered to me and my family, I decided to let the system play out. On any given assignment, I chose to make a difference, and I trusted that my efforts would steer me where the institution needed me most. This mindset paved the way to my selection as the highest-ranking enlisted member in the Unites States—all due to a selfless show of dedication and loyalty.

I recall one instance while serving as a command chief (a fairly senior position as SNCO) and partaking in a so-called "talent management" conversation that was anything but, with a group of more senior command chiefs. The conversation had very little to do with known and demonstrated capabilities. It revolved around what seemed to be "checked boxes" rather than effectiveness and value. As an example, these "managers" refused to nominate highly capable leaders for a position because they "did not have the right exposure and experience," meaning that they had not done their time at a certain level. They placed value on an extremely rigid progression method: if you hadn't served under a two-star general, they would not recommend you for a three-star general assignment. Their gauge was skewed in the sense that they were primarily looking at tenure of different positions and not the impact made during their time in that organization. It was a "good ol' boy" system of taking care of allies and pets rather than capitalizing on true talent within the organization.

When it came time for my next assignment, they gave me some bullshit rationale on the recommendation of what was best for me, which I quickly challenged with facts and the almighty concept of common sense. To no surprise, their counter was shallow in nature and context, insulting even. "Once you make it to our level," they said, "you will understand." What I understood was that each of them was self-serving, carrying out a purely self-beneficial agenda along with everyone else in their so-called circle of trust. In contrast, if you were to ask the people I served with at that time and prior to that assignment, officer and enlisted, they would say I ran circles around these ass-clowns. The same went for some of the other great SNCOs that weren't pushed for certain assignments because of the selfish nature of the leadership at the time.

It was the perfect opportunity to exercise the Silver Bullet in this chapter. Many of us decided to let the assignment system play out, even while influenced by a court of jesters. We committed to proving our worth and making ourselves useful. Long story short, every one of those SNCOs deemed unworthy of certain assignments rose to heights above most of the ones in charge of "talent management" at that time. Adherence to the ethos of a quiet professional, focused on delivering results, displayed the true capabilities of each of those great leaders and, in turn, shed light on the questionable decisions of those who had no business being in charge. Actions, humility, and perseverance spoke much louder than words, and eventually pushed mediocrity aside.

Reporting for duty with the purpose of earning your keep will give you a competitive edge over peers and will enhance your credibility. Do this consistently, and you will always find yourself useful and making the necessary changes needed for the evolution, progress, and positive reputation of the organization.

SILVER BULLET #7

Always leave the workplace better than how you found it.

Organizational pride and reputation are often the drivers of high performance and ease of talent recruitment. Building that pride takes time, and there are two critical variables: the brand and the culture of the organization. People who aspire to join these organizations invest the best of themselves to get in. Once they're in, they tend to go above and beyond to prove their worth and to enhance the credibility of the organization. In doing so, they also enhance their own reputation as a member in good standing. That was the case for me with JSOC. I wanted it bad, and I poured my heart and soul into the selection process for that elite unit. Once I was in, I did not want to let the organization down. With that in mind, I contributed daily to the enhancement of the team.

For some, simply being a member of JSOC was good enough; they were content performing routine tasks (which were far more formidable than most organizations in the world). For others, as in my case, we wanted to live up to the hard work and ingenuity of our predecessors, the warriors who left a mark in the famed history of the command via their contributions of mission capabilities, processes, equipment development, and the modernization of our techniques, tactics, and procedures. During nearly a decade in the command, I witnessed extraordinary feats that drove change for the entire Department of Defense, not from the people at the top but from those in the trenches—those who wanted to add to the maxim of *credibility* being our currency. Everyone loved a fat "bank account of credibility," and we protected our investment at all costs. Being a "quiet professional" was (and is) a badge of honor.

One example is Admiral William (Bill) McRaven. Under the United States Special Operations Command (USSOCOM), Admiral McRaven paved the way for the creation of a program called the Preservation of the Force and Families (POTFF) to enhance the resilience of our organizational human capital. Refusing to be deterred by the highly bureaucratic and painfully slow US government innovation processes, he developed a plan to almost instantly begin filling the voids in care and support for our troops and their families after ten years of armed conflict. Bill's calm and collected demeanor—much like the way he carried himself during combat—led to many battles won in the form of approvals. What he created was not only an ecosystem of care for USSOCOM but also a benchmark process loosely adapted by the entire Department of Defense to better care for our warfighters. He exercised his leadership power to show appreciation for the tough duties of special operations personnel and their continued sacrifices.

When I was assigned to the Pararescue and Combat Rescue Officer school (PJ/CRO) in 2005, I got the chance to emulate

Bill's approach to workplace improvement. Upon arriving, I noticed the students were still wearing the same outdated Vietnam-era gear I had worn in 1996. When I asked the instructors why, they said it was due to a lack of funding from headquarters. We were already four years into the conflict in Afghanistan at that point, and most of these students would likely deploy to perform their combat duty in the months after graduation. We needed to get them good gear, the kind they'd wear in combat, to ensure familiarity with it and, in turn, their chances of success and survival in battle.

The opportunity presented itself when the four-star general in charge of the command would be visiting our military installation, and I was invited to breakfast with him to discuss readiness and training of the force. Prior to the visit, I did my due diligence. I, along with our supply professionals at the school, researched, listed, and priced all of the equipment shortfalls for the gear the men needed. The bureaucracy had been fine with keeping the same outdated gear just to make do. Not on my watch. Against their guidance, I had our supply section place my research in the proper administrative format to expedite the acquisition, and I made several copies to bring to the meeting.

The general opened with a diatribe about training for combat, the importance of realistic training, and ensuring the success of our troops in battle. I saw this as an opportunity to "call the baby ugly" and make him aware of our current gear situation. When he asked for questions from the forum, I raised my hand. "Sir, I agree with realistic combat training, but we are speaking out of both sides of our mouth when we say we fully support that goal," I said. "As we speak, I have Pararescue students training with outdated gear that negates the feel, muscle memory, and configuration they will be issued for combat," I continued. "In fact, I wore that gear over a decade ago, and I find it negligent that after four years in combat operations, we have not upgraded to today's technology."

"I was not aware," the general said. "Can you give me some examples?"

I proceeded to show him photos of the current gear, letting the visuals speak for themselves. I then slipped the folder to him and his assistant. "Here are the proper items that we need to meet your training goals and to ensure their combat effectiveness," I said.

"Consider it done and expedited," he said.

The folks at headquarters were not happy—I got a world-class ass-chewing from the commanding officer—but it was a risk I needed to take for the sake of our people. And I was willing to take that risk. When we received funding from the general to expedite the purchase of proper gear, the same people who chewed my ass were now crediting themselves for the improvements, but I didn't care. JSOC made me into a quiet professional, and this was all about our people, not about me. The culture of an organization and its leaders can have a profound impact on the actions and courage of its people. And it was only possible because I was a proud member of that organization.

The high cost of personal sacrifice, the famed reputation of the organization, and the pride of being a member created a highly competitive environment. Honor was the psychological salary of each member, and action was the expected behavior of those proud few. But in order to make our pride work to the advantage of the workplace, we needed to espouse our values with those of the organization. In such an environment, you must take full ownership of your task, project, or duty while casting aside biases and deeply rooted personal beliefs, making *sacrifice* another form of currency. In Silver Bullet #4, regarding amateurs versus professionals, I spoke of the discipline and dedication required to master any task or project. In JSOC, that was the basic expectation for action. We were there to do whatever the nation needed us to do. The culture of JSOC was widely known, understood, and easily bought into.

Culture is not built overnight. It is a slow-moving train that utilizes each stop on the route as an opportunity to validate itself by delivering action to the right place, at the right time, by the right people, while often onboarding new talents, thoughts, and ideas that promote improvement and innovation. Once culture is calcified, it is increasingly difficult to change. It takes one of two things to change an organization's culture: a prolonged effort, or a crisis. A prolonged effort provides the time, consistency, and validation of the changes needed. A crisis quickly validates failures and gaps, and it ignites the survival mechanism of that prideful culture to sustain their reputation and good standing. Both scenarios create opportunities to add value to the organization. Both provide an arena to test capabilities and validate assumptions, but most importantly, these scenarios create a forum for lessons learned via immediate feedback.

The JSOC feedback mechanism for improvement is brutal, something called "after-action reports," or AARs. These fact-finding sessions are candid, honest, and pointed to identify issues or actions that fall into three categories: sustain, improve, or discard. AARs are an opportunity to highlight successes and failures, ownership and responsibilities, and validation or elimination. The openness and flatness in these forums not only create a transparent environment of communication but also emphasize the responsibilities of each member and the proper accountability for their actions. Upon completion, mistakes rarely reoccur and successes are briefly celebrated. But the valued outcome is the direction to improve or discard actions, decisions, or processes via experimental actions to validate our capabilities. That is how we left the workplace better, and it was a daily chore for all of us.

The organizational leadership must provide an environment that welcomes ideas, criticism, ingenuity, and ownership. People in JSOC are empowered to create and validate capabilities, with due credit in the end. After leaving the command and joining other organizations, I brought this mentality as a means to enhance the culture of each organization with the goal of simply leaving the organization better than how I found it. That approach does not have to be exclusive to the Tier 1 operators at JSOC. There are many other military units that exercise the same amount of pride with their assigned missions, but they all have something in common: the need for improvement and a disdain for the status quo.

The same goes for the business industry in the private sector. Companies like Google, Amazon, Apple, and scores of others have cultivated that culture that lends credibility to their brands and products. Leaders must be open to the ideas of others, and visionaries must be courageous enough to experiment, unleashing the power of innovation in the quest for improvement. The opportunity for improvement is present in every echelon of any given organization. Open communication, solid interpersonal relationships, and appreciation of the work of your people open the door for discovery, learning, and innovation.

Engage in transparent dialogue, hold brutally honest feedback sessions, and take ownership of your responsibilities—then watch your organization transform. But keep in mind that one cannot go at it alone. Diversification of the thought processes of an organization comes via inclusion of outliers, differences in opinion, and different levels of experience to cover every possible option. The more courageous we are in our actions, and the more open-minded we are, the more likely we will be to make revolutionary contributions to the workplace.

SILVER BULLET #8

The true aim of an education is not knowledge but action.

English philosopher and psychologist Herbert Spencer once said that "the great aim of education is not knowledge but action." This resonated with me the moment I read it in 2002, at Camp Alpha in Bagram, Afghanistan. I've met people who have more degrees than a thermometer but lack common sense. I have met scholars for whom the mere notion of stepping out of academia rivals the fear of a declawed cat released into the wild. You can only talk your way out of so many things in life. Most of the time, you'll need some sort of action to back it up. This is where the Carnivore leader fine-tunes a balance between the two: having not only the brains but also the guts to be an example for others to follow.

In my original leadership paper, I wrote that it is not what we know but what we do that matters. In Chapter 5, we spoke about the Silver Bullet of adding value when speaking, not time. Now, you must back up the spoken word by physically exemplifying what you talk about. The value of learning is critical to proper decision-making. The more you know, the more you will consider when making decisions. Knowledge helps you eliminate blind spots and spark curiosity toward the unknown. But education alone will not help you maximize your full potential. You must put your mettle to the test.

Education comes in many forms. It is not exclusive to sanctioned or accredited institutions that provide a diploma after you meet their requirements. Using my career as an operator as an example, I didn't earn an associate's degree until my sixteenth year in military service, and I didn't earn a bachelor's degree until my twenty-sixth year. But that doesn't mean that I wasn't enriching my mind with the proper information. You see, I spent my time during my formative years learning how to be the best PJ I could be. That was my profession, and I took it seriously. I spent many hours researching successes and failures in rescue operations. Much of that occurred via reading a lot of manuals, books, and studies. Additionally, I was required to maintain my credentials as a paramedic through the National Registry of Emergency Medical Technicians, which occupied a lot of my time, not only with studies but with practical skills. The same was true for rescue operations. My classroom was the operational environment, my professors were the experienced operators overseeing our training, and my diploma was defined via mission success. My brain, being a muscle itself, completed just as many reps as my biceps in the gym. There was no stagnation on daily growth, and that was my priority at the time.

But being so operational-focused created an unhealthy bias against "school." I often frowned upon military members who spent the majority of their free time working on degrees that had nothing to do with their military career. For a long time,

I refused to honor the value of a college degree, partly due to my success as an operator without it. I admit now that I was ignorant at times in my rhetoric undervaluing education. It wasn't until I finally decided to enhance my own academic acumen that my eyes were open to the value of knowledge. When I decided to pursue a degree in higher education, I chose something that could help me be a better leader and manager. My position as a senior enlisted leader required me to execute at an exemplary level to set the standard for our subordinates. It was then that I regretted not doing it sooner, and I wished that I could take back everything negative I had said before about higher education.

After completion of my degree, I saw immediate improvement in my research and problem-solving abilities. I expanded my vocabulary and understanding in many areas. My education helped me engage in enlightening conversations outside of the operational environment, with people I often had nothing in common with. Most importantly, it helped me think more clearly and deeply about the actions I took. People often address the "say-do" gap, referring to those who run their mouths and do nothing, but what I gained as a benefit of higher education was a bridge to cover the "know-do" gap. For twenty years, I had proven that I had the physical ability to do things that few would dare do, but now I had the knowledge to contemplate my actions and to better understand my surroundings.

A life best lived is one that is well-rounded, a life with not only physical prowess but also the knowledge to achieve any task while thinking through the problem. This balance keeps you from being taken for a fool, and your propensity to take action will help you demonstrate and validate life's teachings.

In my case, I wasn't educated to memorize and pretend; I was educated to understand and take action. I've strived to become a "common sensei" of the book smart, and an igniter of motivation for the physically capable. As a leader, I have sought to help others balance knowledge and action to be more effective.

Educate to perform, not to pontificate. It is what you do, not how much you know, that makes the most difference.

SILVER BULLET #9

Never ask anyone to do anything you are not willing to do yourself.

"The old man did it. Now GO ON, you ______ . . ."

Those were the words of a young Pararescue student during a rock-climbing rescue demonstration while I was the commandant of the PJ school. I was the "old man" he was referring to. Some of the students were struggling with the task of scaling an overhang on a vertical climbing wall, a very difficult and physically draining evolution if you don't apply the proper technique. "It's impossible," they said, so I showed them that it wasn't. I demonstrated the task by performing it myself. Afterward, I spoke to them about the proper technique to conserve strength and energy while climbing, followed by a walk-through of the problem, step by step. The above is one example of the many times I have chosen to do things versus watching or just talking about them. I chose to be a living example of the expectations levied upon our people. My actions helped shift the students' mindset from impossibility to competition. They didn't want to let an old man show them up.

As far back as I can remember, and still to this day, I've embraced the challenge of being in the arena. Demonstration has always followed explanation in my life, the two being inseparable from each other. Always up for a challenge, I've done many things that most humans would shy away from. As I mentioned in an earlier chapter, I've been tased, pepper-sprayed, and bit by military working dogs. I've waded through sewage, been punched in the face, climbed through tunnels and other confined spaces, and endured many other unpleasant scenarios to experience what my subordinates were tasked to do, or to fully understand the worst-case scenarios of my own duties. The thrill of uncertainty has always outweighed my fear of failure. For that reason, I have never shied away from getting in the arena to gain an understanding of a task through experience and, in turn, not letting my people down.

In Silver Bullet #3, I spoke of the senior leader who wanted to save himself for his PT test. In the interest of self-preservation, he proceeded to let down hundreds of troops who wanted to "embrace the suck" with him.* It was a colossal failure on his part. That day, he failed to lead by action, likely due to a lack of confidence in his own physical readiness. I felt ashamed for him, embarrassed that he held a leadership title in the organization, and I doubted he could ever save face with that group. The "leader" did not rise to the task.

After that missed opportunity, his credibility sunk to a level lower than amoeba shit. He exhibited a lack of courage to lead

---

* Sarah Sicard, "The Origin of the Military's Iconic Mantra: 'Embrace the Suck'," *Observation Post*, July 19, 2022, https://www.militarytimes.com/off-duty/military-culture/2022/07/19/the-origin-of-the-militarys-iconic-mantra-embrace-the-suck/.

by example. He made the poor choice of remaining a spectator, standing on the sidelines in his crisp, starched uniform like King Shit of Turd Mountain while the rest of us were muddy, sweaty, and even bloody. At the culmination of the PT session, he came to tell the troops what a great job they had done and ask how it went. "You should've gotten that pretty uniform dirty, Chief," one of them answered. "Then you wouldn't have to ask." I added that he should probably deploy a search party to recover his reputation and his credibility. He missed a great opportunity that day, but his troops also learned a great lesson: an example of what *not* to do as a leader.

Actions do in fact speak louder than words. A habit of leading through action provides the ability and courage to accept short-notice or no-notice challenges. The mere act of acceptance with little to no knowledge of what's at stake will earn you immediate credibility, even if you come up short. It's an empowering thing to do as a leader. It offers your subordinates an opportunity to showcase the pain they go through, and it shows how much you appreciate the duties they endure to meet the demands of the organization. It also provides you with knowledge so you can later speak from experience. But to do so, you must have confidence in your own physical abilities. There is no time to "save yourself" when the opportunity arises; all you can do is save face. You must have the confidence to try, but you must condition your body to withstand any challenge.

Just as demonstration should follow explanation, action must always follow a challenge. A combination of action and intellect develops inner courage, or as we say in special operations, having the guts to try. Do not stand on the sidelines while your people are in the arena. Choose to be side by side with them to properly lead them and build team camaraderie. In the end, a leader has to be both physically and mentally ready to serve as an example of the culture and expectations of the organization.

SILVER BULLET #10

Where there is a choice to be made, there is a lesson to be learned.

Our future is shaped by the choices we make today. Whether it is a positive outcome or a negative experience, they both have equal value:

Courage + Action = Experience

This equation has been the story of my life. I have made good choices and bad choices, and every one of them has served as a lesson. A William Shakespeare line from *Hamlet* goes something like this: "There is nothing either good or bad, but thinking makes it so." In tandem, Will Rogers once said, "Good judgement comes from experience, and experience comes from bad judgment." These two quotes have helped me navigate the personal struggle of learning to live with the decisions and choices I make. They've offered me a mechanism for thinking deeply about choice, consequences, and ownership of my actions.

A lesson in bad judgment came early in my military career. I had only been in for a year when I was disciplined for behavior unbecoming of a military member. Reverting to old habits, I got into an alcohol-related incident that led to a demotion, loss of pay, and a tainted reputation—not such an awful outcome, considering I was nearly kicked out of the service. The embarrassment of being in that position, especially in such a small installation where everyone knew each other, was crushing. My motivation plummeted, it impacted my self-esteem, and I questioned my purpose for joining. All I had wanted from the military was discipline and structure, and I had failed miserably. I had deviated from the expectations of the United States Air Force.

I thought my military career was over. After enduring my punishment, many people told me I was done and that nothing good would come with a blemish like that on my permanent record. I started believing that narrative and almost parted ways with the Air Force. I felt sorry for myself. Then, one interaction turned it all around. A sergeant who wasn't in my immediate chain of command noticed the change in my behavior. I was no longer the outgoing jokester airman she had grown accustomed to seeing around the base. One day, as I was heading back to the barracks to eat my ramen noodles for lunch, she called me over and asked a critical question. "What are you doing moping around the base like the world has done you wrong?" she asked.

My reply was typical. I was in denial, refusing to take responsibility for my actions. "It wasn't my fault," I said, along with some other bullshit about how I was a victim in the whole ordeal.

"What did you do wrong?" the sergeant asked. "And what are you going to do about it?" I just looked at her, bewildered. "You don't have to give me an answer today," she said, "but if you want to dig yourself out of this hole, come by my office tomorrow morning, and we can discuss a plan of action."

Her simple questions got me thinking more deeply about my situation. Looking back, I know wholeheartedly that was exactly what she had intended. I went to my room, and as I ate my lunch, I thought about what she had said. When I went back to work, I wondered why no one in the section had approached me the way she had. After all, these were the people in charge of me. Had they been fine with my change in demeanor, unconcerned about whether I improved? That evening as I went to bed, I thought about it even more, and I decided to take her up on her offer to help turn the tide of my misery.

When I arrived at her office, she handed me a piece of paper. "I'm glad you came," she said. "You're not a bad kid, and I believe you have great potential and a place in the Air Force." She pointed to the paper, which had dates and numbers on it, among other things. "This is a plan highlighting the goals you must meet to get back on track for promotion and financial recoupment. It'll help you account for your actions with humility," she said. "Follow this, and you'll be fine."

I decided to be accountable and own my way forward. I made sure never to forget the shame I had felt after letting myself and many others down, and I carried out the sergeant's plan without compromise.

The lessons I learned from that unfortunate incident, a situation I could've evaded, allowed me to help others. It deepened my capacity for empathy and my ability to relate to others. One might even say it offered me extra credibility, the "been there, done that" kind—although it's not the kind of credibility to be proud of. What I found is that if we choose to find positivity even in negative spaces, we can make use of any scenario. As a leader, there came many instances where it was my turn to help people in despair. Openly discussing my own transgressions helped garner a sense of trust and buy-in from recipients of the advice I offered. As I progressed through the ranks, my transparency gave others hope for overcoming failures, and confidence to move forward, because they knew I was looking out for them. In every case, I advised them to learn and never repeat their mistakes. I also asked them to pay it forward, to make it their duty to do the same for someone else. This cycle of helping others has been the most rewarding effect of using lessons learned. The joy and satisfaction of doing so is something that has always fulfilled me as a human.

It is always good to explore options in life, and it is also good to "fail forward," a phrase popularized by John C. Maxwell.* Options are opportunities for growth and learning, and the options we choose help curb our biases and broaden our experiences. Once you choose to take any particular course of action, the key is to switch to a learning mindset. This is where your courage, followed by your actions, builds your knowledge and understanding, and also your credibility. Have the courage to act decisively and assume risk to gain experience. Risk-taking raises awareness of one's limitations and capabilities. Not all things in life will be pleasant; what really matters is that we learn from any given situation. There is value in every experience, so recognize the outcome of your actions, take ownership, learn from it, and move on.

---

* John C. Maxwell, *Failing Forward: Turning Mistakes into Stepping Stones for Success* (Nashville: HarperCollins Leadership, 2007).

Never underestimate the power to help others based on your own experience. Using the lessons you've learned, you can relate to others, and you can expedite the collection of resources to aid them. More importantly, you can place others at ease by letting them know they're not alone, and that others have overcome the misery they are experiencing. Be humble enough to display your vulnerabilities. Be courageous enough to show your imperfections to others. Be diligent in the act of following through. Be a dependable role model for your people. You can build all of this upon the foundation of your trials and tribulations.

SILVER BULLET #11

Luck is when preparation and opportunity meet.

When it's "go" time, you don't have time to get ready—you must always be ready. I learned this lesson while involved in combat operations. When every choice counts, you do not leave your destiny to chance. You must deliberately take control to the greatest extent to mitigate the dangers surrounding you and your team. In critical situations, there is no such thing as luck. There are only actions, reactions, and adjustments. And the outcome depends on your courage and preparation: courage to enter the dragon's lair, and preparation prior to slaying the dragon. For those who believe in luck, which I obviously do not, I ask that you consider the above and think about those situations in which you considered yourself "lucky." Was it because of something you did? Was it because of something someone else did? I am sure someone's actions, reactions, or adjustments played a part in the outcome.

In our Tier 1 community, the purpose of training was to make sure we left nothing to chance, as discussed in

Silver Bullet #4. The hard work, dedication, and diligence of a professional in the quest for excellence is what drives results, earning the classification of "elite." But this is not exclusive to combat. The same goes for anyone who decides to dedicate their life to becoming an expert in their field of passion. Consider, for example, baseball player Derek Sanderson Jeter and rock climber Alex Honnold (baseball and rock climbing are both passions of mine). Jeter didn't pull off five World Series wins by relying on luck, and Honnold didn't free solo climb El Capitan merely by chance. Both were deliberate in their quest to develop, test, improve, validate, and prove their capabilities.

In Jeter's case, according to his autobiography *The Captain*, the skinny kid from Jersey and then Kalamazoo, Michigan, always wanted to be a Yankee. His love for baseball and his strict upbringing shaped the Hall of Fame shortstop from an early age. His parents were uncompromising in instilling values in both Derek and his younger sister, Sharlee, making them sign contracts every year that outlined acceptable and unacceptable norms of behavior. His mother, to instill a positive attitude in her son, insisted that he refuse to use the word "can't—which is something I wish more parents would do nowadays. In the Jeter household, they were taught to earn their way into their desires and aspirations, and if they deviated, they dealt with the consequences.

Alex Honnold was shaped by a different dynamic. His childhood household, while not as strict as Jeter's, allowed him to be creative and to dare to accomplish. At an early age, he frequented a local climbing gym in Sacramento, California, many times a week to perfect his technique. During that time, he never thought of himself as a bad climber, but he also never considered himself great. Being aware of his surroundings, he noticed the strength, agility, and technique of other kids in the gym, something he at times considered a "natural gift." He realized it was a gift he didn't have, so he put in the sets and repetitions to match a higher skill level. Upon the death of his grandmother and the divorce of his parents, he often skipped school to boulder by himself, to clear his mind by doing something he was passionate about.

There is a common trend between these two great athletes. At the tender age of four, Jeter declared that he would become the New York Yankees shortstop, and he began marching in that direction. It is my belief that such a drive and focus to achieve his goal led to his success as a ballplayer. The proof is there, as it is in Alex Honnold's case, who started climbing at age five according to an article in *The New York Times*.* As an adult, Honnold could've afforded a decent home if he wanted to, but for him, what represented freedom was living in a custom-outfitted van with a kitchenette, cabinets full of energy bars, and climbing equipment. Think about the consequences of not having the commitment to achieve his goals. One misstep during any of his climbs could have ceased his existence. He had no choice but to be ascetic in his study, training, and testing of the climbing routes before free soloing. This often came with countless hours of frustration, pain, disappointment, and repetition.

In both cases, we have a commonality of learning, practice, commitment, standards, courage, perseverance, and resilience.

---

* Daniel Duane, "The Heart-Stopping Climbs of Alex Honnold," *New York Times Magazine*, March 12, 2015, https://www.nytimes.com/2015/03/11/magazine/the-heart-stopping-climbs-of-alex-honnold.html.

Within both world-famous personalities, there also exists a high sense of humility and self-respect. This humility and self-respect, coupled with the credibility built via their accomplishments, defines their classy approach not only to their sport, but also to life. This passionate drive to accomplish high-stakes feats led to record-setting deeds and enshrinement into their respective professions' record books. This is also true for industry giants such as Bezos, Gates, Walton, Jobs, and the list goes on, where the above attributes along with creativity led to great success.

I also have something in common with Jeter and Honnold. I grew up working for what I needed, wanting to be a man of action from an early age. I joined the military to facilitate my independence and satisfy my attainment of a purpose in life. I defeated the odds during the Pararescue training pipeline. I set my sights early in my military career to become a Tier 1 operator. I knew I wanted to serve for thirty years, and I knew I wanted to become a chief master sergeant, the top 1 percent of the force. I could never have accomplished any of this without personal responsibility, ownership, perseverance, and courage as described in Silver Bullet #2. But it was the habits I developed in the quest of my goals that led to even more precious accomplishments. To become the highest-ranking enlisted member in the most powerful military in the world is a byproduct of a consistent and honest approach to proving your worth in life. It has nothing to do with luck.

"Lucky breaks," as some call them, are also not about luck. Lucky breaks are simply the positive results of the few who believed they could accomplish something—the ones who didn't shy away from a challenge or choose to play it safe. The courage and fortitude exemplified by the "doers" often garners criticism from naysayers: "He was in the right place at the right time" or "She just had the right boss to push her along." But these are not the true reasons why doers shine. That "right place" is the opportunity, and that "boss" is often the one who, at some point, will vouch for your credibility. They are merely factors in a bigger scheme, one that attests to your character.

Regardless of which professional path you choose in life, the outcome must be driven by your actions, the tackling of opportunities, or acting on something others did not. Taking control of any given situation is the essence of carnivore leadership. You go and get it; you don't wait for it to come to you. Frame your success by always having a primary, alternate, contingency, and emergency (PACE) action plan. Trust me, it works in combat, and it'll work for you.

SILVER BULLET #12

Image is a first impression; daily demeanor is a lasting impression.

After graduating from the PJ training pipeline, I knew what I wanted to do for the rest of my life: to be a PJ and save lives. My dedication was unflinching and consistent, and I performed to the best of my abilities. But simply being a good PJ was not enough; I needed to be a professional. The habit of abiding by US Air Force standards of dress, appearance, fitness, customs, and courtesies provided a solid foundation to build upon. Our appearance was to be clean, neat, and serviceable. We were to maintain an optimum level of fitness, ready to perform and survive in any location our country required us to be. We were to carry ourselves with respect, loyalty, and honor—not only while in uniform but every day, on and off duty.

A true professional balances intellect and abilities, not only to project the right image but also to perform at a level that builds credibility. I learned this early on. Chief Master Sergeant Wayne Fisk and Technical Sergeant John Kingsley—former marine and my immediate supervisor at the time—taught me to always be presentable and proper in appearance. Not only did we need to be physically fit to perform our duties, but we also needed to silently project PJ expectations by exceeding Air Force standards and promoting warrior culture. Attention to detail was a requirement: tying a tie properly; wearing matching shoes and belt; knowing the difference between formal, business, and business casual attire. This all helped promote a professional image to make a solid first impression, followed by a professional demeanor that properly represented us as warriors and gentlemen.

Throughout my thirty-three-year journey as a special operator and leader, I mentored others to better present themselves, take care of their bodies, and enhance their performance. Some followed through, while others ignored the advice. My approach was simple: play by the rules, do your part, and strive to be better than your peers when competing. I was surprised at how many saw this as revolutionary advice. A little bit of sacrifice and habit goes a long way.

In Silver Bullet #3, we discussed the importance of staying in shape and alluded to the benefits of a proper image when marketing ourselves for opportunities in the job market. Unfortunately, some people think they can fool their way into opportunities. Posers, con men, and infiltrators have something in common: they pretend to be something they are not, to profit or deceive. Short-term impressions are easy to maintain, but long-term impressions are only sustained via one's character, capabilities, potential, and consistency.

Long-term pretending is seldom sustainable. For those who oversell their capabilities and attempt to live a lie, exposure is inevitable. We can deter these scam artists through diligent talent management and proper screening of personnel. In JSOC, our assessment and selection processes were extremely rigorous to prevent candidates from faking their way into the organization, a risk that the nation could not afford due to the scope of responsibility of such an elite unit.

An initial assessment of a person's capabilities requires that they look the part, act the part, and be the part on a consistent basis. By assessing image, one can get a sense of the discipline, energy, and self-respect of an individual. By witnessing their actions, one can gauge their skills and abilities. By analyzing their image, consistency in actions, and behavior over time, we can get a good sense of whether a person is who they say they are. If they fail to perform based on their responsibilities, then an employer can take action to remove the individual or even demote based on their exaggeration of their capabilities.

Let's discuss image—the physical appearance and composition of a person. A fit person has certain attributes that attract employers. Fitness demonstrates discipline, health, and self-care. It also indicates self-respect, availability, and longevity. I will even dare to say that health impacts the financial decision of some employers if healthcare is part of the package. Good health is a good selling point for any industry because it highlights you as dependable and present for your duties and responsibilities. That is not to say that every organization must fill their rosters with Cross-Fitters and disregard those who are obese, or not so fit, as they tend to be the majority nowadays. I am by no means body shaming those who are not fit. I'm simply highlighting the benefits of a fit person. If you are not fit, however, I do encourage you to consider adopting a better lifestyle for the sake of those who love you and for your tenure on this planet.

When it comes to recruiting and talent acquisition, fit and intelligent people are rare. Any manager of talent must be cognizant of the value of individuals with the right blend of intellect and stamina when they present themselves. These rare individuals can certainly be a deciding factor in the success of any organization, if they are offered the opportunities and empowerment to rise up to any challenge. In order to gauge and sustain a competitive edge in those individuals, accountability must be ever present to prevent setbacks or regression.

Demeanor and consistency are part of that required depth for sound credibility. The way you treat people, the way you choose to be a learning entity, and the way you show your worth to the organization are all essential in demonstrating your credibility.

Because first impressions are critical for gaining access to leaders, jobs, and promotions, many mediocre people take the "fake it" approach to create a perception of greatness. "Faking it" often leads to failure on the part of both the member and the organization. First, the faker often falls short of expectations that the organization assumed to be within their scope. Second, the organization fails when it must fire or demote the faker, which can hinder the organization's progress. In the leadership context, promoting and empowering these people can lead to organizational turmoil, fractured relationships, lack of progress, and marginal profit.

Fakers are often low on potential and high on ambition. They're the greatest ass-kissers of the organization and the biggest examples of sham, flash-in-the-pan rock stars. Hiring and retaining such people often spoils morale and weakens the reputation of the workplace. For example, let's highlight the many social media pretenders seeking "influencer" status to make a quick buck. They create an illusion of appearance, knowledge, expertise, and counsel that is often shallow and unvetted. But this con-man practice is nothing new; it has existed since jobs were created and interviews became an employer's way to seek talent. The sad part is that many employers fall for this illusionist trap. Image might get your foot in the door, but it is consistent performance in the arena that serves as a gauge for your capability and potential.

SILVER BULLET #13

Heroism is of the moment,
but professionalism is a constant.

I spent nearly twenty years fighting and being involved in the global war on terrorism in the Middle East. I often witnessed humans doing extraordinary things, many of them earning awards for valor in combat. Their actions, at crucial moments in their service, gave them a badge of honor that automatically enhanced their credibility, reliance, and willingness to go above and beyond. But not all carried themselves as professionals in other facets of life.

Ever heard of the saying "Never meet your heroes"? Well, the same goes for some decorated warriors. We all have flaws, even the most valiant among us. Sometimes we allow our accomplishments to go to our heads, alienating us from those who look up to us. For some of us, a moment of bravery becomes a script for the rest of our lives. I am not saying there's anything wrong with celebrating such feats. The problem is when people use their moment of valor as a crutch to get them out of unethical or even criminal behavior, or use it for self-gain.

Remaining stuck in that moment, without follow-on actions to help others, is not an honorable thing to do. On the flip side, there are those who perform in that moment of great risk, and then make it a mission to add value to society by helping others cope with adversity—to tell a story of patriotism and sacrifice, and to set others up for success.

Our living Medal of Honor recipients are a great example of this. I have had the honor to serve and know many of them, living and dead. One common attribute among them is humility. These men are very in tune with that prestigious symbol around their necks. They are also in tune with the price of earning such an honor. They have to consistently relive the horrible scenarios that placed them in a position of do or die. They must remember the faces of fallen comrades who perished, often second-guessing themselves, pondering the many "what-ifs" that might've brought someone home alive. They are forever tied to what happened in that moment, ever reflecting on the many possibilities for a different outcome, or how different life would be without the spotlight that now follows them everywhere they go.

In my warrior opinion, even though they are national treasures, they are not consumed with fame or glory; they are instead very approachable. Take Staff Sergeant Leroy Petry as an example. As a member of a Ranger helicopter assault force conducting a daylight rotary wing raid in the vicinity of Paktya, Afghanistan, Staff Sergeant Leroy A. Petry "distinguished himself conspicuously and with gallantry and intrepidness" on May 26, 2008. He risked his life, going "above and beyond the call of duty" during "an extremely close and violent engagement with an extraordinarily determined and well-armed enemy." Here's a little more about Staff Sergeant Petry's actions that day:

> *During the initial engagement, Staff Sergeant Petry was shot through both legs and another Ranger was hit by enemy fire. Shortly thereafter, an enemy hand grenade landed amid Staff Sergeant Petry and two other Rangers; despite his serious leg wounds, Staff Sergeant Petry unhesitatingly moved to the grenade, grabbed it, and immediately threw the armed grenade away from his fellow Rangers. The grenade detonated shortly after Staff Sergeant Petry threw it away from his fellow Rangers resulting in a catastrophic amputation of his right hand and multiple shrapnel wounds penetrating his body. This deliberate individual act of heroism by Staff Sergeant Petry saved the lives of his fellow comrades and allowed the completion of the mission.* *

One afternoon as Leroy and I walked the halls of the Pentagon, we walked past an Air Force officer with a cast boot on his left leg. In his ever humble and genuine approach to talking with people, Leroy asked the man what happened. The officer, oblivious as to who he was talking to, offered a humorous response, something along the lines of playing ultimate frisbee. Observing the bright-blue ribbon and distinctive medal around Leroy's neck, the officer asked what happened to Leroy, focusing

---

* US Army official website, "Medal of Honor: Sergeant First Class Leroy A. Petry, Operation Enduring Freedom," accessed March 17, 2025, https://www.army.mil/medalofhonor/petry/.

on his prosthetic arm. Leroy's response was one for the ages. "Ah, not much man," Leroy shrugged. "Just had to chuck a grenade." The look on that poor officer's face still makes me laugh, and so does Leroy's response.

Better than laughter is the lesson Leroy taught me that day. By a simple act of humility, he showed me what compassion looks like in its purest form. The way he responded to the officer's question showed me the importance of not comparing one's hardship with that of others, and how important it is to empathize with what troubles other people. And lastly, how important it is to not let the successes of the past carry you for the rest of your life. Leroy lives each day looking for solutions to the troubles of others, much like he did that fateful day in Afghanistan. His character, consistency, genuineness, and compassion are at the core of what a professional must be. He is not stuck in the past; he thrives in the present to create a better future. He is a perfect example of the right blend of heroism and professionalism, and I love him like a brother for it.

What we can learn from remarkable humans like Leroy is to never rest on your laurels. Instead, utilize your experiences to add value to society. Each one of us is experiencing something at this very moment. Make that experience a page in the encyclopedia of your life, with the intent of helping others improve, and be introspective in your actions. Give someone the opportunity to create favorable outcomes not only for themselves but for those around them. Continue to pay it back, and be a leader in every sense of the word.

SILVER BULLET #14

Loyalty is not mindless obedience.

America is losing its sense of unity. Far-right and far-left political practices have fractured our love for one another in places where Red and Blue are separate teams in a daily death match for supremacy. Elected officials are often the best-of-the-worst choice between mediocre options, and they add fuel to the fire, further dividing our citizens. It seems political campaigning has shifted from what a candidate can do for the American people, to how a candidate can smear the character of their opposition for the sake of popularity and votes; this happens on both sides of the aisle and in news narratives. It has become a bona fide shit-show and often a source of global mockery.

Being an apolitical entity in my three decades of service to our nation, I learned to embrace the good that each party brings and call out the dividing agendas that are far from the middle of the aisle. In my opinion, the "middle" is where most of our politicians should be; they should be capable of collaborating with one another to create a positive outcome for American citizens. "We the people" is slowly being replaced by "We the party," mostly via blind followership of some members on each side of the aisle. This practice of taking things at face value versus digging into the details and facts has crippled our system and negatively influenced the minds of many. We do not have to be this way. We must take the time to analyze and understand opposing views and rationally state our differences, all without fracturing relationships.

Being loyal does not mean being a blind follower. I once believed that loyalty was the foundation of trust. I later realized I had it backwards. Developing trust and having confidence in organizational leaders is a conduit to loyalty. When people believe wholeheartedly in the direction of an organization, loyalty is attained. One problem I've seen too often is when the ambitious blindly follow just to meet their personal goals and facilitate their agendas in a selfish manner.

People seldom abandon or disregard causes that enhance their lives, especially those that benefit them or help them grow. If the people of an organization have a purpose, a cause to fight for, and an environment that allows them to work toward those goals, productivity is often at its maximum. As a leader, one must set the standards that promote such an environment. Then, once the standards are set, the leader's job becomes the continuous improvement of the organization to consistently oblige to those expectations. Consistency is key. People must make it a habit to perform according to the standards a leader has established.

If an organization has set standards, the guidance and expectations are clear, and accountability is in place, the organization can then effectively measure its success. Feedback from this kind of measurement can generate further opportunities to improve or sustain individual and organizational performance. As people make this method their norm, that is when loyalty sinks in and their potential is unleashed.

In my time at JSOC, expectations and standards were widely known based on the reputation of the command. Every candidate in our assessment and selection process, also known as Green Team, understood the expectations of the command. If a candidate fell short of those expectations, nine out of ten times there were no questions or rebuttals; it was very clear. Each candidate had one goal in mind, and that was to live up to the actions of the past unit members who built, enhanced, and inculcated the expectation of nothing short of excellent. It was that loyalty to JSOC's reputation that drove each candidate to perform to the max of their abilities each day during selection, and each day as a graduated member of that rigorous process. None of them wanted to be the one to tarnish its reputation. That, ladies and gentlemen, is a pure example of organizational loyalty, and trust and confidence in its leaders.

I have seen this in other organizations where there is a strong sense of culture. For example, some associated units that weren't part of JSOC exhibited an equal level of loyalty. While they weren't a part of the crucible of Green Team, they assimilated to the expectations or the organization for the following reasons: first, the historic reputation of JSOC; second, the track record of mission success of the organization; and third, the credibility of the people within the organization.

Reputation, consistency, and credibility are critical to the immediate buy-in of the culture of the organization. The fourth critical variable is performance accountability. There is nothing more motivating than the risk of losing credibility once you enter an organization that you respect and value. This is one of those cases where fear of failure actually serves as a positive. It keeps you sharp, it keeps you in check, and it keeps you focused on your purpose. It is this kind of person that tends to be the most loyal and dedicated to the organization. They believe in what they are doing, they believe in their leaders, and they believe they are part of something greater than just their actions.

They do not blindly follow. They contribute to the overall success of their workplace. They know their own value, and their leaders recognize it. They reap the informational benefit of transparency and inclusion. They achieve daily growth by testing their capabilities, validating their assumptions in a risk-friendly environment, and they possess a sense of ownership of their tasks. A true leader never blindly follows the hierarchy and never expects blind followership from subordinates. Both leaders and followers must validate why they are to trust, and why they should be loyal.

Remember, facts, knowledge, and comprehension of any given situation always lead to intelligent conversations. The opposite—assumptions based on social media, soundbites, headlines, or unchecked comments—leads to the moronic state of division we experience today. We must do better, and we must be well informed.

SILVER BULLET #15

Bad habits are like a comfortable bed: really easy to get into and really hard to get out of.

Bad habits, we all have them. They often create stress, shame, and even fractured relationships. A conduit for comfort and laziness, these habits tend to be more popular than disciplined hard work. They lead to procrastination and failure to act. Self-awareness and acknowledgment of the bad habits that affect us are the best prevention mechanism. We might refer to some of these bad habits as "falling asleep at the wheel," "sedentary practices," or "barnacles on the ass of progress," to name a few. The fact that we have several monickers like this speaks to their commonality among humans.

I remember vividly the days prior to September 11, 2001, when most of us took freedom and safety for granted. Americans had a tendency to bury their heads in the sand regarding the possibility of conflict on our own soil. This horrible habit, a sense of entitlement when it comes to freedom, was likely the biggest shock factor during the attacks on that fateful day.

How could this happen to us? How dare anyone do this? Well, it happened. And there we were, getting ready to strike back in one of the longest armed conflicts of recent times.

Not surprisingly, on September 12, the day after the attacks, awareness replaced a habit of complacency. Volunteerism replaced a habit of entitlement, as many Americans grew eager to serve. An immeasurable sense of pride emerged in favor of our Star-Spangled Banner, our military troops, and our first responders. "United We Stand" became a national motto, not only in words but in action. In short, the tragedy on 9/11 awakened the sleeping (or complacent) giant.

While addressing the anniversary of the September 11 attacks on LinkedIn in 2023, I urged both military personnel and our citizens to not let our current safety become a blanket of ignorance in a comfortable bed of complacency. It is human nature to embrace the pleasantries of comfort. Therefore, we can assume that stepping out of one's comfort zone will raise anxiety and generate stress to a certain extent. Why would anyone want to abandon a state of such contentment? This is well for mental health, but sometimes we give in to bad habits in the quest for such comforts. Too often, we enter the realm of comfort, and we cave under a fear of the unknown.

I've seen this fear of the unknown—this fear of failure and a lack of confidence—hinder progress and growth in talented individuals. It was at those moments when the quote about bad habits being "like a comfortable bed" resonated with me. At the time that I wrote the quote in my Moleskine book, I was often sleeping in makeshift shelters, and even in the dirt, in Afghanistan. Upon arriving at Bagram Air Base in 2002, my accommodations were a tent, a cot, and a sleeping bag. Our bathrooms were a PVC pipe dug into the ground as a urinal, and a confined plywood shack for a shitter. Our showers were in another tent, often rendered useless due to the moon-dust dirt of Afghanistan that left you looking like a sugar cookie once you opened the flap and walked toward your sleeping quarters. Meals were less than desirable, but necessary for performance in combat.

All personal luxuries were absent. I missed my comfortable bed and the controlled climate of my home in North Carolina. I missed the warm presence of my wife and dogs. I missed the ability to let my guard down and drift into oblivion. But then, I would come back to the reality of the present. Where I was at the time. What my duties were. And the consequences of not fulfilling those requirements. It was clear to me and my teammates that in combat, comfort was a luxury, not a requirement. The great unknown would be our oyster, and discomfort would be the norm.

With time, we developed habits to embrace what we called "the suck," which translates to a life surrounded by misery, hardship, sacrifice, and harsh accountability. "The suck" was the norm, and we adapted to not only survive in it but to thrive and learn from it. It made us tougher, more confident, more resilient, and more appreciative of the lives we were fighting for. You are very welcome, America. Safety, freedom, and liberty are great causes to fight for, especially when our loved ones reap the benefits of our sacrifice.

There's another side to this equation—the reciprocal "suck" of the families we left behind. As we shot people in the face in combat, our families slayed the dragons of daily life. Their "suck" was more complex than combat. Life in combat is simple: find the enemy, capture or kill it. On the home front, our families dealt with home maintenance and cared for our kids, pets, and other family members. They balanced personal careers, school, and emergencies. They worried about the unknown whereabouts of their warriors. They worried they might never see us again. Throughout twenty years of combat, our families back home had the toughest task of all, and they embodied the greatest example of sacrifice.

Military families must adapt to many crises. The comfort of being rooted in a neighborhood for many years, attending the same schools, being with the same friends, and even being around immediate family are often not a part of military life. The hardship required of military families makes tough and resilient individuals who thrive in uncertainty. Their habits come from being accustomed to discomfort and living in uncertainty.

Comfort zones are for the complacent, for those who dare not deviate from their routines. The complacent continuously fail to explore possibilities and validate the combination of emerging talents and knowledge. In short, comfort zones are for the lazy and meek, the Herbivore's Zen den. Since the beginning of time, there have been individuals who dare to attempt what the masses refuse to do. We call them "explorers," "pioneers," "warriors," or "heroes." To discover the things others wonder about. To set new stages for generations. To ensure the progress of civilization. Leadership courage is no exception. This exploration leads to a sense of awareness and validation, but most importantly, it leads to the betterment of mankind.

There are some who view accountability as hostility when it comes to correcting bad habits and preventing complacency. While serving as the SEAC, I wrote a post titled "Accountability Is Not Hostility." Here's what it said:

You are hostile toward me because I am different. Having personal differences is irrelevant to having common standards. In the military, all members have prescribed rules of conduct, appearance, and performance that are more demanding than those of society. But lately, a trend of subversive disregard of standards seems all too common across the force.

People often castigate accountable leadership as a way to justify their lack of adherence to known rules and expectations. "You are discriminating" or "You are toxic" and even "You are disconnected from this generation" are bumper stickers on the vehicles of the mediocre, headed down a one-way road to failure.

What people dedicated to service need to embrace are the sacrifices required to fulfill our duty to our nation. We give up quite a bit of our personal desires and comforts in order to be the defenders of freedom. Leaders who care for their people and have a responsibility for their well-being, reputation, and combat effectiveness will always account for deviations of standards in order to ensure the discipline of the force.

Do not mistake accountability for hostility. Instead, be self-reflective and accountable, and do what is required of you before placing the blame on those who are doing the right thing.

As leaders, the best way to avoid developing and repeating bad habits is to correct and account for infractions on the spot. Popularity seldom corrects the wrong, and leaders must subscribe to the fact that they can't be all things to all people, but that they can always be more to their people. In the end, a leader must act on the side of right rather than popular. Be principled, be tough but empathetic, and be a living example for the change you want to see.

SILVER BULLET #16

A life without humor is like a book without words.

I grew up in a household where laughter was free and available. Both my parents were extremely witty and creative. Their jokes were easy to visualize and quick to tickle you. In addition to their sense of humor, we watched humorous shows, many with iconic Latin characters of the era such as El Chavo del Ocho, El Chapulín Colorado, Cantinflas, and Machuchal, to name a few. We read funny books and told funny stories. With my cousins Jamal and Sahim, we created funny radio shows containing content that was beyond our years, and we shared the gift of humor with everyone around us. Lacking an abundance of possessions, we filled the void with the gift of joy. As I reflect upon those times, I now realize it's when I began to understand the meaning of the line from Hamlet that I mentioned earlier: "Nothing is either good or bad, but thinking makes it so."

Fast-forward to 1993, when I volunteered for Pararescue duty. While undergoing training at the OL-H (PJ school), I was given the collateral task of being the Team Cartoonist. While this may sound simple and fun, the repercussions of not putting full effort into those cartoons often had catastrophic consequences—not only for me but for the entire team. The Team Cartoonist, in essence, was the deciding factor between a hard day versus a horrible day.

The quality and humor of the cartoon would often set the tone for each day. If the cartoon didn't live up to the expectations of the instructors—if they perceived it as lazy, shitty, or lacking some sort of factual reference—the team would work harder that day, a painful experience on top of the hardship of an already challenging curriculum. Conversely, if the cartoon was deemed high-quality, humorous, and based on actual events, the cadre would exercise some lenience in the amount of pain they imposed on us. The task was about a lot more than just putting pen to paper. It required critical thinking, factual (or exaggerated) recollection of the previous day's events, and a sense of what the instructors would find humorous. It required extra mental effort and some sort of artistic talent to contribute to the well-being of the team. I exerted full effort into every one of those cartoons, most often landing on the good side of the instructors' expectations.

The cartoons were a long-standing tradition of the school. I'm not sure if this was by accident or by design, intended to create a culture of resilience via laughter, but that's exactly what the cartoons did for us: they pulled us through hard times and helped us connect not only with each other but also with our instructors. Today, as prospects roam the halls of the school in hopes of becoming a PJ or CCT, those cartoons serve as a historical reference of our daily happenings and the shenanigans of the course. One might even say they serve as an intelligence-gathering source on the expectations of the program, and the critical times where instructors did their best to break us.

Cartoon drawn by CZ during his time in the important role of "Team Cartoonist" at the Pararescue selection course.

In a few cases, the cartoons backfired. Sometimes it was the tone of the narrative. Sometimes it was the depiction of the instructor. But often it was a combination of the two that brought the most anguish upon us. In one case, I chose to highlight an instructor's inability to keep up with us doing push-ups. For the next two hours after the instructors read the cartoon, we experienced unimaginable pain during a run with that same instructor. Come to find out, all the other instructors found it funny, but not him. I'm not sure if he was scheduled to run us that morning, but there he was. I'm a little sick to my stomach as I write this, remembering that grueling morning.

We certainly paid the price, but we gained more than just an ass-kicking that day.

When I presented the cartoon to the team prior to taking it to the cadre, the majority found humor in the truth it depicted. The instructor was a professional and we all highly respected him, but that didn't absolve him from our cartoons. In fact, like a group of inmates challenging an unjust warden, that small win of doing more push-ups than him showed us that we could at times best even those who had the power to select us as their future teammates. We found humor even after the ass-kicking we received. Often the best experiences in life come at a high price; that day, our wallets were empty, but our souls were strong.

Later in Bagram, in 2002, began the longest combat streak in US history: the Global War on Terror. Prior to deploying, team shenanigans ran rampant. From man-to-man challenges to cage wars, nothing was off limits. Man-to-man refers to reciprocal actions for a prank pulled by the opposing party. Cage wars refer to the act of pulling pranks on those who fail to secure their equipment cages, often by placing undesired items in them. An equipment cage is a five-by-eight space where all the tactical equipment of a special operator is kept. If left unsecured, it was free game.

In one case, an operator left his cage unlocked, and the team filled his CamelBak hydration backpack with goldfish. Another time, an operator went to many unlocked cages and held an industrial-sized magnet near all the wallets, erasing their credit and debit cards. Sometimes, a perpetrator would empty half the opposing party's toothpaste and replace it with Lidocaine gel, numbing the victim's mouth. Needless to say, humor played a big part in coping with the daily turmoil of being a special operator.

In Afghanistan, we used humor as a source of relief from the many stresses of battle. We also used photos, board games such as Balderdash, and songs to bring a smile to the souls who otherwise slowly darkened day by day. Death, suffering, uncertainty, pain, and many other harsh difficulties prevailed during those times. But the laughter and camaraderie helped remind us who we still were on the inside: human beings who wanted to do good for mankind.

After eighteen years of on-and-off involvement in combat, I had to get help for my mental and physical injuries. When I arrived at the National Intrepid Center of Excellence (NICoE), I wasn't sure how my treatment would go. Was I worse off or better off than I thought? Would I be red-tagged (meaning unserviceable) upon completion of the program? Would it make any difference at all in my life, and help me save my marriage? Day by day, in the company of my peers experiencing something similar to me, I did my best to remain open-minded and to look critically at myself. And then art and humor came back once again to save the day.

One of the greatest experiences of my inpatient treatment at NICoE was art therapy, led by Mrs. Adrienne Stamper. While we tried many other avenues to release stress—yoga, counseling, and meditation to name a few—art was the one that helped me channel my inner demons and allow that humorous guy inside me to breathe again. Adrienne used a mix of conversation, art techniques, and music to help me find my safe place. A place where I could finally be honest about my emotions and catalogue my rights and wrongs. It was in those moments where I felt the most. It was during those times that I came to see the hope of improvement.

I'm still not sure if the cartoons during the Pararescue training pipeline were there by design or by accident, but one thing is certain: they were therapeutic and still are to this day. As I write this, just a few days ago, I sent photos of those cartoons to some of my old teammates, and their responses said it all:

"Dude, I can't quit laughing."

"I'm about to piss myself."

"Don't show that one to my wife."

"Holy shit, those were great times."

They really were great times. It was a time when we found purpose in our lives, a time when we put our mettle to the test, a time when we found a family we never expected—a time when the nation built a future bench of defenders of the US Constitution. Laughter can serve as a rope ladder for exfiltration, or in layman's terms, a rope ladder for getting the hell out of the pit of darkness. Humor, if you can find it, can help you climb to unimaginable levels of success, and catapult you into the life you should be living.

SILVER BULLET #17

Know the difference between "character" and "reputation."

The correlation between character and reputation is intertwined within the fabric of anyone's credibility. When I interviewed with General Milley for the position of SEAC, he was aware of my reputation. Our time spent during the interview was to catch a glimpse of my character and to validate the things people had said about me. What he found was consistency of narrative, which meant validity of character.

Knowing yourself is a valuable tool to build a solid reputation. Your interactions with people of all walks of life, regardless of what you can gain, are planks that eventually become bridges for opportunities and collaboration. In my case, I treated junior service members the same as I treated the generals, admirals, bosses, and executives. To me, humans were humans. Some had better opportunities and had achieved success. Others were learning and figuring out a path to excellence. And some were simply existing or beat down and just needed a little motivation to get them going. In all cases, I saw an opportunity to lend a helping hand.

One example was an interaction on a rainy Monday morning with a junior airman in Okinawa, Japan. That week, I had been slated to speak at a First Term Airman Center (FTAC) course on what twenty years of military service had taught me. At the time, I was the most senior enlisted member of that post, and interaction with our junior members was common. As I was heading to the FTAC building, I drove past this young man, stopped, and offered him a ride to get him out of the pouring rain. He accepted and got in the vehicle, oblivious of who I was. I introduced myself simply as CZ.

When I asked him where I could drop him off, he said he was in the FTAC class. "Great," I said. "I'm headed that way too. Perfect timing." Based on my age, I'm sure he assumed I was senior, but because I wore rain gear, my rank wasn't immediately visible to him. When we arrived, he thanked me for the ride, and I told him that I would see him there shortly. With a puzzled look on his face—likely due to a lack of recognition of who I was—he dismounted the vehicle and went into the building.

As the sergeant introduced me to the class of airmen as the command chief of the base, I noticed the young man sitting at a table in the second row. His eyes grew big. He then leaned over to the person sitting next to him and whispered, louder than he likely intended, "Holy shit! That's the dude who gave me a ride—the chief!" I couldn't help but chuckle as I took the stage to talk to them. I could just feel the wheels turning in the airman's head, wondering what the hell had just happened. I then presented my points of discussion before opening the floor for a question-and-answer session.

From those who knew me, the questions were about my time in combat. One young man asked bluntly, "How many people have you killed?"

"Wouldn't you be more interested in how many lives I've saved?" I asked.

I then went on to explain the mental tax of taking lives in combat—a stark contrast to the excitement of killing characters in a video game. While my warrior reputation preceded me, it also sparked a conversation to help squelch the group's initial fascination with the glory of war, and instead lead to an understanding that every one of them needed to be ready to take the fight to the enemy when the opportunity presented itself.

The young man who received a ride from me stood up then. "Why did you choose to give me a ride this morning when many other cars just drove by and didn't acknowledge my existence?" he asked. I told him that regardless of who he was or the position or rank he held, I simply saw a teammate in need. The rain was pouring down, and I wanted to assist in any way I could. He deserved a better start to the morning than to arrive soaking wet to a classroom with thirty other people. In short, it was the right thing to do.

A few years later, I received an email from the young man, asking if I remembered when I gave him a ride in the pouring rain. I said of course and asked him how he was doing. He had received two promotions since that time, and went on to tell me about the impact of that interaction in Okinawa. After that morning, he said, he had researched who I was, and he couldn't believe how humble and down-to-earth I was. He said it was in that moment that he found a role model, someone to look up to. From the classroom conversation about combat to the kindness I had shown him, he said that he had a lot to live up to, and that he would seize every opportunity to lend a helping hand. He closed by saying that I had lived up to my reputation via actions, humility, and kindness. That note provided me with a humbling sense of satisfaction knowing that I was living in accordance with the purpose of my life, to help others be better than I ever was.

While we can benefit from a solid reputation, we must never forget that in order to retain that credibility, one must meet expectations via actions. There are many other stories from people across the Department of Defense, their families, and civilians who spoke a story similar to that of the young airman in Okinawa. Back to the General Milley interview, after concluding our conversation, he proceeded to check in with the people who had served with me, to make an informed decision on whether I was the right person to hold the office of SEAC. Unknowingly, by being a consistent helper of people, my reputation provided an edge in a very tough and honorable competition to become the United States' highest enlisted leader.

A key attribute of leadership is empathy. Helping others in the manner that you would like to be helped is a very honorable act. It must become part of your muscle memory for action. Much like accurate marksmanship is necessary in combat, humble acts of kindness must be ever-present in your daily routine. Simply be decent to others, and you'll set yourself apart from a majority who disregards this critical human quality. Like Janet's forearm tattoo says, in the words of Arthur Freed, "Don't try to be different, just be good. To be good is different enough."

“

SILVER BULLET #18

A promise made is a promise kept.

This is by far one of the toughest Silver Bullets to live up to, especially the more senior you become in your leadership role. When you're in charge, people expect results. When they ask you for something, they expect you to deliver. Keeping promises is important for relationship building, and when time is limited, a leader must prioritize which actions to take. In my position as the SEAC, nothing pained me more than falling through on an ask from our troops. I hated to say no. The volume of requests, the frequency of travel, and your own life issues create the inevitability that something will fall through the cracks. To prevent catastrophic failure, we must be in tune with our capabilities and limitations.

So how do we work on maximizing our span of influence? Something I found helpful was the use of digital reminders to follow up on the many requests from our force of 2.4 million people. I used a program on my phone and computer to assign priority, context, deadlines, and reminders to help me "rack and stack" my daily chores and asks. But even with an effective system, we're bound to miss some. Much like everything in life, perfection is nearly impossible. Maintaining a balance that favors the wins, not the losses, is the sweet spot for any leader. But even then, one big loss runs the risk of overshadowing the many small wins. As leaders, we must categorize, analyze, and prioritize our actions.

Prioritization is critical in maintaining your credibility. Doing only the things you can do and delegating the rest is a great start. Delegation can serve as a multiplier to achieve desired results, to provide experience to your teammates, and to help them enhance their own credibility. Regardless of whether you take on the task or delegate it to a teammate, follow-up, accountability, and closure are the test of your effectiveness. But keep in mind that delegation doesn't absolve you of responsibility. If it's asked of you, you own it. If you're unable to deliver, it reflects upon you.

Take a look at your reliability track record. Gauge how many people see you as a reliable promise keeper and how many have been disappointed by your failure to take action. Continuously validate your method of accountability and promise-tracking. Keeping a promise is not just about delivering the expected results; sometimes you will be unable to do so based on conditions surrounding the issue, outside parties who have the authority to make things happen, and time constraints associated with the task. In the end, whether you deliver or not, your people must know that you did everything in your power to answer their call.

In combat, my promise to the war-fighting joint team was the Pararescueman's Code:

> *It is my duty as a Pararescueman to save life and to aid the injured. I will be prepared at all times to perform my assigned duties quickly and efficiently, placing these duties before personal desires and comforts. These things we (I) do, that others may live.*

When one follows this mantra line by line, it is easy to account for the expectations levied upon you by your team. The reason this mantra works is because it is pointed, specific, concise, and attainable based on the known skills of the executor. My teammates knew what to expect from me. I knew what to expect from them. And I promised them that I would always give it my best to live up to that promise with a no-fail mindset. Falling short of this promise could mean the inability to save someone's life, to bring them back home to their families, or not being ready when the call to danger came.

My teammates knew I was skilled, reliable, and diligent. Even when I was unable to keep the wounded alive, there was never a question of my skills, motivation, and execution. Sometimes circumstances prevent us from being victorious. In combat, the enemy always got a vote in the outcome of any given situation. But the confidence my teammates had in me, coupled with a consistent level of performance, gave them faith that I could respond to crises when the chips fell, just as I had confidence in them to watch my back and provide a security bubble around me and the patient in any situation. Regardless of the outcome, every promise was kept, because everyone lived up to the professional expectations of their duties.

I'm human, so sometimes I've fallen short. I've forgotten to add an event to my calendar, or forgotten an important date in someone's life. There have been times when I've failed to send a congratulatory note, or missed attendance to an event, or allowed a request for a congratulatory video to fall through the cracks. Talk about a horrible feeling, having to contact those people afterward to apologize. I've also been on the opposite side of the equation, where a leader promised to be in attendance at my events with fellow enlisted leaders but failed to show up, without ever apologizing or acknowledging their faux pas. So I've chosen to own these failures and not make excuses, as I considered myself negligent in following up.

Regardless of the situation, in peacetime or wartime, if I failed to keep a promise or overlooked a request, I resorted to honesty and owned my failure. No excuses, no lip service, always offering an opportunity to make it up. Honesty and ownership go hand in hand. Even if damage is done, honesty can help sustain the relationship and keep the door open for future collaboration. In the end, be cognizant of your capabilities and limitations; do not overpromise and underdeliver. Be surgical in your method of accountability, and build a team around you that has the knowledge, skills, and an attributes to pick up your slack. Be diligent in execution and thorough on closure. And most importantly, be honest if you're unable to deliver. Your credibility advertises your reputation. Let your promise-keeping score be one that enhances your credibility.

SILVER BULLET #19

Time management is a waste of time. Concentrate on "action" management instead.

Time waits for no one. Time does not negotiate. Time does not care. Time, therefore, is your most masterful foe. In today's digital society, it's easy to lose the fight against time. The many distractions, options, social media scrolling, and amusing but valueless videos consistently rob us of our most precious resource: time. Knowing that time will never wait, for anyone or anything, vectors us away from time management and toward "action" management instead.

The year was 1993. Along with many other hopeful young men, I sat near the Chaparral Pool at Lackland Air Force Base in San Antonio, awaiting my turn to complete a training evolution called "buddy breathing." This exercise required a team of two trainees to enter the water sharing only one snorkel. We were to remain underwater, our faces submerged, and share breaths by passing the snorkel back and forth. The objective was to remain calm when dealing with contingencies (in this case, sharing one air source), and to trust your teammate. But there was a catch. While performing this exercise, an instructor would enter the water and do everything in his power to steal the snorkel, break the teammates apart, or make one or both of the trainees break through the surface for air. Any of these would mean a failure for both trainees.

To pass the training evolution, the team had to endure three minutes of chaos underwater while braving the instructor's interference: splashing, prying the snorkel from the firm grip of the trainees, trying to break the trainees' hold on each other, occluding the hole in the snorkel, submerging the team to "steal" a breath, or even a punch to the gut. This evolution was notoriously the end for many, and we knew it. Each trainee team had to develop a strategy to deal with the mayhem of those three minutes (which seems like an eternity when you're underwater), or risk washing out.

Being comfortable underwater wouldn't make the time go any faster, but being aware of the actions one could take in those three minutes would give you a better gauge of the finish line. For example, I knew I could hold my breath comfortably for at least one minute. I knew the instructor would enter the water five to ten seconds after the trainees did. I knew that if we were submerged, it usually lasted for no more than ten seconds. And I knew that it all had to come to an end at some point. Being aware of the actions one could take in those three minutes and being aware of the options that were in our control often led to success.

In combat, the same applied. Often, we had a good idea of how much time we could spend on a target before enemy reinforcements would show up. That calculus drove the expediency of actions and the prioritization of tasks, and it helped determine when to call the mission off if the risks were to outweigh the benefits. The actions you could take were far more important than the time you had to take them. This motivated the team to be on the top of their game. It forced flawless collaboration and synchronization among the units involved, and it often drove success in highly complex and risky mission sets.

Think about your day and the time you have to do your work. Now account for the time taken for small talk, internet searches, coffee breaks, and so on. Then, account for the countless meetings imposed by your organization, and throw in family contingencies. Is your day already a wash? What about your task list, email queue, and phone calls? Getting stressed already? Well, peace of mind is just a few habits away.

Discipline is at the forefront of action management. A structured routine for accomplishing tasks, like many other experts have stated before, is key to staying on track. I explored many methods to track my actions, and through trial and error, I fine-tuned my approach to effectiveness. If I had fifteen minutes or less, I could tackle some emails that needed attention. My emails were color coded to show me which ones were directed at me, courtesy copied, or just for information. I also used that time for follow-up phone calls. When I had thirty minutes, I concentrated on meeting prep for the following day. If I had sixty minutes, that was creative space to develop presentations, talking points, etc. While these are just a few examples, I wanted to provide context into the actions one can take, even with "limited" time. Do this long enough, and you will develop a productive habit of actions and a bias for such.

SILVER BULLET #20

Lead people with dignity and respect at all times.

We live in a hostile world where insults have replaced criticism. A place where the average human reaction is fueled by skepticism versus the benefit of the doubt. A place where hostile behavior is almost an expectation, a factor to anticipate when drafting communications and preparing for engagements. A megaflow of information fuels this, and influencers—good or bad—capitalize on it. The digitization of information has made communication more complex and blurry. For nondigital natives like me, it has been easy to revert to the old ways of gathering facts and not get spun up based on immediate and often nonfactual news or messaging. I consider myself an optimist, but also a realist that relies on facts and trends to prevent falling victim to someone's spin of reality.

I was late to the game. I didn't start using social media until around 2016. My apprehension was based partly on my adherence to a mindset and ethos of the "quiet professional." I was also skeptical about its value, mainly due to the abundance of buffoonery, disparaging and critical comments, and the volume of misinformation mistaken as fact. To me, it was counter to acting with dignity and respect toward others. And if you can't act with dignity and respect, then you can't lead with dignity and respect. Even after I finally began using social media, I chose to minimize the negative noise by posting only professional narratives to help others be better. I found out quickly, however, that when you are an enforcer or advocate for rules, trolls come out of the woodwork to criticize you.

The digital courage of the trolls has always amazed and amused me. Never have I seen so many dipshits getting their rocks off from engaging in online debates. It's easy to hide behind a pseudonym and a keyboard, seizing every opportunity to violate the value of dignity and respect. Several times, I've invited them to engage in an actual conversation to better rationalize the issue. To no surprise, most trolls decline, but the few who choose to engage adopt a different tone, a more submissive approach to the narrative, and a more reasonable consideration of the topic once they receive additional information versus their sole biased position. Funny how reality steers people to do better.

In a society that is quick to cancel, replace, and upgrade, we have lost the art of appreciation for things that work. In simple terms, for things to work, one must put work into them. Take marriage, for example. It's not always roses and smiles, but if your spouse is worth it, you will find a way to get to a fix on any given issue. Janet and I have been apart for half of our relationship. Deployments, training, and work have required a lot of travel, leading to my absence. Lack of consideration for each other's needs or lack of awareness for each other's priorities created turmoil in the limited time we had together. But with time and experience, we learned to better communicate and understand each other's situation, and to enjoy and appreciate the time we had together. This work within my marriage also helped me improve my leadership style at work, where I developed positive habits to consistently treat people with dignity and respect.

When you grow accustomed to working through issues without easily giving up, you develop that lost sense of appreciation—you learn to shun the hostile culture that has become so prevalent. These habits play heavily into fostering dignity and respect in the workplace while making you a more effective leader. They force you to rationalize and think through the issue without shooting from the hip.

It is extremely difficult to open doors with a closed mind, and an open mind is critical to leading with dignity and respect. One of the worst actions you can take is to disregard the input of your people by thinking you know what is best. Curbing your bias helps you not only to see the many variables in any issue, but also to learn from the talents of others. This inclusion helps foster trust and appreciation, creating a healthy dynamic in the workplace. I've seen both sides of the equation in our government, in the military, in industry, and with interpersonal relations. On the good end, those who are inclusive and open to ideas create a strong following. Conversely, those who are narrow-minded and egotistical gain only the disdain of their folks and only the support of their token ass-kissers. In the end, the ones with a strong following are the ones worthy of the honor of leadership.

Mistakes, setbacks, and even failures are bound to happen. When they do, a good leader can choose to turn adverse outcomes into lessons rather than regrets or accusations. As previously stated, accountability is not hostility. Lessons help us grow and own our outcomes. The more we own our actions, the more effective we will be as leaders. And if ownership becomes the norm for an organization, we are bound to be more productive in the long run by creating a respectful and dignified culture and brand. This habit and culture will ultimately help ensure accountability across the board.

CONCLUSION: TAKING CHARGE

When I first heard the Carnivore versus Herbivore analogy from my Navy SEAL teammate Jim Hintzke, I was intrigued, amused, and enlightened. It made sense. There are those whose make things happen and those who wait for things to happen. Really, there is no in-between. My motivation to spread the word aligns with the qualities of a Carnivore: actions, not words; consistency; and selflessness. This was my habit throughout my military career and my life. All with the ultimate goal of being a loyal, dedicated, and dependable teammate. Realistic expectations were always at the forefront of every project or task, operating fully aware of our surroundings, never with our heads buried in the sand.

In the movie *The Matrix,* the Delphic Oracle offers the protagonist, Neo, advice regarding his purpose, and then, as a gesture of kindness, she gives him a cookie fresh out of the oven. She then points to a quote on a sign over the doorframe that reads "Temet Nosce," which translates in English to "Know Thyself." The conversation had been centered around Neo's need to let go of his fears and limitations to reach his full potential as "The One." But even after the conversation, as he takes a bite of the warm, fresh cookie, Neo still has doubts. He thanks the Oracle for the cookie, and he leaves. Later, he must choose to take either the "red pill" or the "blue pill." If you're unfamiliar with the Wachowski Brothers' film, the blue pill would keep him in a fantasy world; the red pill would bring him back to reality. Even better, think of it this way:

Blue = Bullshit
Red = Reality

In real life, there are no blue or red pills, only experiences derived from our choices and actions, or lack thereof. In combat, as we navigated our actions, choices, and decisions, we first gauged the conditions often set by our enemies, mitigated by our confidence in our capabilities and trust in one another. Never in my time in combat with my US Air Force, Navy, and Army brothers did I question their skills, capabilities, and loyalty. No matter the situation, it was clear we'd have each other's backs. Personally, I had an oath and creed to live by, and I'd be damned if I were to let them down.

There is a reason the year 1993 is consistently referenced in this book. That was the awakening of my spirit, the birth of my purpose, and the time to take control of my life. For most of my professional career, my purpose was to take care of people. I was quick to figure out that the path to leadership was paved by credibility. You cannot earn credibility without demonstrating abilities. You cannot develop or validate abilities without putting them into practice—putting them to the test. And to put abilities and talents to the test, you must have courage. Once you establish credibility, the doors open for leadership opportunities. And once you go through those doors, you must always meet the expectations of those you serve. Consistency in your approach to leadership matters. When leading, you must be of value to your people. Often, when I wrote, people would read. When I spoke, people listened. When I acted, people watched. But this didn't happen because of the position I held; it was due to a long-lasting record of speaking no nonsense, calling out mediocrity, and standing up for what's right. Having their attention and receiving their feedback was a self-assessment of my effectiveness as a leader.

With a poor leader at the helm, an organization can only gain an advantage against an organization with a leader who's even worse. Your one job as a leader is to take charge. There will always be naysayers. Negativity will always find an opportunity to infect the organization. You must be the antidote to prevent the infection from spreading. You will be criticized, and often you will not be popular, but you must uncompromisingly always do right—not right based on bias, right based on facts. And you must have the courage to stand up to anyone, up or down the hierarchy, that goes against the good of the organization, the well-being of your people, and the moral and ethical behavior you exemplify and expect from those in your charge.

You deserve what you tolerate. You must stand up against the actions that have a negative effect on your life. This is how you develop the courage to speak truth to power or perpetrator. This is how you stand up for yourself, your family, and your teammates. If you get just one thing out of this book, let it be the courage to start taking charge instead of taking shit. Hooyah!

AFTERWORD: TWENTY SILVER BULLETS

As I was growing up in the remote coastal mountain range of Western Oregon in the early 1950s, our spartan villages along the Siuslaw Watershed were wild with youth transformed into US Marines. Fresh with American victory in World War II, we children never tired in playing games reliving South Pacific battles at such locations as mysterious Saipan or valiant Iwo Jima.

Most households didn't have television back in the mountains in those days; it hadn't been perfected yet. So we entertained ourselves by faithfully listening to radio programs, especially on Sunday evenings. There was *Fibber McGee and Molly*, Groucho Marx, *The Whistler,* and especially *The Lone Ranger*. All sense of time ceased when he came on. *The Lone Ranger,* aside from being a great, rip-roarin' cowboy program, taught us morals and values, right and wrong, ethics and fairness, pathos and honor. It was "parent-approved" in every household of the area.

And fittingly, to ensure we boys and girls grew up morally strong and appreciative of the greatest nation that had just vanquished—simultaneously—two terrible foes, the Third Reich and the Imperial Forces of the Empire of Japan, the Lone Ranger would bestow upon a deserving character in his radio program a silver bullet symbolizing purity, wisdom, sagacity, courage, and honor. As children, we may not have understood the fullest conveyance of the moral message at program's end, but I remember a feeling of overwhelming satisfaction that I had learned something of an important life lesson from the Lone Ranger, and that my ammo belt of learning was becoming fuller. I felt he and I had a special relationship, and perhaps we did, for many of his principles seem to have guided my life.

When I became a warrior for my nation through US Air Force duty in Southeast Asia and had accrued years of service in "the blue uniform," I would often relay this story as a teaching point at enlisted Professional Military Education (PME) functions, promotion ceremonies, and time-honored military dinings-in. I would explain that we in the United States military use the term *bullet* because we're defenders of our nation and people, and we go after our enemies with bullets. Since our Department of the US Air Force service color is silver, as are our un-battle-dressed aircraft, and qualification wings, and uniform buttons, we use "silver" bullets, I hope, with great wisdom.

Real leaders in the USAF do not use the proverbial pearls-of-wisdom metaphor to keep us safe and free; pearls are too soft and fragile. We aren't. We use bullets: hard-core, in-your-face, no-return-necessary, you-asked-for-'em, devastating bullets. In truth, we use Silver Bullets with all their implications of morals and values, right and justified, ethics and fairness, pathos and honor, strength and deterrence, just like the Lone Ranger.

Many years after retirement, I had the pleasure of meeting

CZ. And it's been Pete 'n' Putz—or Dink 'n' Donk—ever since. Over the years, I relayed the preceding Afterword comments and thoughts to him under various circumstances. He, intuitively astute and perceptive, grasped them immediately, the ever-present Moleskine notebook snapping open, pen flying across the pages as notes were taken double-time. He was always like that, constantly soaring, with wonderful mentors who believed in him. *Aim high*, they'd advise, and he did; there was no ceiling to his sight picture.

I have a document on my computer dated 2012. It is one of the earliest evolutions of what is now in your possession. It remains, essentially, intact and unchanged from that date. Adages remain adages and are remembered because they are time-tested and proven. Their characteristics are specific, relevant, timely, measurable, and obtainable; the only updates required are those to make them germane to the moment, if at all.

The sagacity of CZ's *Carnivore Leadership* is not in dispute. Your success will be directly proportionate to your application of commitment and Silver Bullet #2. It will be a *commitment* (a Carnivore mindset) versus an *involvement* (an Herbivore's mere passing thought). Remember, his guidance is (a) specific, (b) relevant, (c) timely, (d) measurable, and (e) obtainable (or adaptations thereof). As my father advised me when we resided in Alaska in the early 1960s, "Son, as you grow up in this world, there will be times when you'll need to be as imposing as a bear." (He often equated human life to the majesty and beauty of wildlife.) "When those times arise, I want you to have the commitment and courage of a grizzly bear" (Carnivore). Be the grizzly. CZ is bequeathing to us his lifetime of observation, practice, action, and advancement. Where he observes or suffers the brunt of poor leadership, he calls out the offense.

CZ expounds this straightforward, heads-up, to-the-point, logical form of take-charge, lead-by-example leadership. There is no substitute. Something else my father iterated during that grizzly bear analogy: he said that while I would encounter bear-like people in life, when pressed or confronted, they may lack the resolve of the grizzly and possess only soft features of teddy bears, or perhaps Snuggle or Pooh bears. He advised that there would be times when only the resolve and/or leadership of being a grizzly (a Carnivore leader) would suffice. Father's words have served me well, and I find that these principles expounded here by CZ are equally wise and beneficial.

Leaders cannot be Carnivore leaders if their heads are down in the grass or up someone's—or their own—backside. A Carnivore leader has their finger on the pulse of events, their nose to the scents in the air, ears to near and distant sounds, and mind attuned to their people. CZ gives us twenty adages—to suit our fancies—on how we can be better, more effective, and successful leaders.

I have been astounded during the many years that I have known him at his ability to detect a perception, analyze its potential, and reap its rewards. I enjoy his gracious, no-nonsense ways of saying, "Let's win, together!" He's never forgotten his roots of life. From his childhood beginnings in Puerto Rico to entry into the US Air Force and a career-long service in Pararescue, he has been a leader serving people. And *nothing* slows down that service. This was demonstrated in 2023. As he was delivering his speaker's remarks during his formal Relinquishment of Duties speech as Senior Enlisted Advisor to the Chairman of the Joint Chiefs of Staff in Washington, DC, a member of the

National Honor Guard fainted in ranks.

Collapsing fully forward on his face, it was CZ, speaking at the microphone, who immediately sprang to the fallen marine's side before any of the on-site first responders could act. Within the near-minute it took before they arrived, CZ was already attending to the injured man. Then, satisfied they had control, he returned to the microphone and calmly resumed his address. It was a flawless definition of CZ (Silver Bullets #6, #10, and #20).

This is the real man, the real prescription, the real solution (Silver Bullet #7).

Good luck.

—Wayne L. Fisk
CMSgt (Retired), USAF
career Pararescueman, Son Tay Raider,
LSO (last shooter out) Southeast Asia War,
entrepreneur

APPENDIX: TWENTY SILVER BULLETS, ANNOTATED

1. IF YOU WANT TO FLY WITH THE EAGLES, DON'T HANG AROUND WITH THE TURKEYS.

We are products of our environment. Ensure association with successful and motivated personnel, and stay away from the naysayers and slackers. Attitudes are very contagious; exude a positive attitude and set the tone for others!

2. THE PATH TO SUCCESS IS NOT EASY, CHEAP, OR QUICK. IT WILL REQUIRE GETTING UP AN HOUR EARLIER AND GOING TO BED AN HOUR LATER.

Paying attention to detail, ensuring quality, and striving for excellence are all time-consuming tasks that are also taxing on the mind and body. However, the positive outcome of hard work and due diligence makes every second spent on any given task well worth it. Quality control is less painful and much easier than damage control.

3. THE BEST WAY TO STAY IN SHAPE IS TO NEVER GET OUT OF SHAPE.

Get accustomed to an active and healthy lifestyle. It will make you more energetic, create a positive mindset, and give you utmost confidence. It also provides a proper military image. We are the nation's warriors; let's look like it and have the energy to do what the nation asks of us!

4. AMATEURS TRAIN UNTIL THEY GET IT RIGHT; PROFESSIONALS TRAIN UNTIL THEY CAN'T GET IT WRONG.

Always strive for perfection. Keep in mind that in the United States Air Force, we execute a NO-FAIL mission. This applies to everything we do: garrison, combat, and our families. This is our core value of "Excellence in all we do." We must maximize every opportunity to make ourselves better, so we can, in turn, teach others to be great. Practice and hard work makes perfect. Continuous and constant proper execution brings us excellence.

5. NEVER PASS UP A GREAT OPPORTUNITY TO SHUT THE HELL UP IF YOU HAVE NOTHING PRODUCTIVE TO SAY.

Speak when adding value to the subject of the conversation. Learn to listen when you have no input; do not get in the habit of loving to hear yourself speak! Lastly, remember that you do not have to attend every argument you are invited to. Silence is sometimes golden and classy.

6. WHEREVER YOU GO, THERE YOU ARE— SO MAKE YOURSELF USEFUL.

Always find a way to exist and earn your keep. Never deny a helping hand to those in need.

7. ALWAYS LEAVE THE WORKPLACE BETTER THAN HOW YOU FOUND IT.

Our goal in life must be to continuously improve all things we come across. This continuous improvement is imperative to ensure the success, advancement, and the positive reputation of our organization. Set up your replacements for success. Leave your mark everywhere you go!

8. THE TRUE AIM OF AN EDUCATION IS NOT KNOWLEDGE BUT ACTION.

Use the hours spent in the classroom as a means to plan for action. Our main goal is to lead the charge when presented with the opportunity, not to talk about it. Remember that it is what WE DO rather than what WE KNOW that matters most!

9. NEVER ASK ANYONE TO DO ANYTHING THAT YOU ARE NOT WILLING TO DO YOURSELF.

The best way to gain loyalty and trust from your personnel is to let them know you care about what they do by experiencing it yourself. I have always chosen to "do things" versus "death by PowerPoint" when getting familiar with a squadron's assigned mission (unit immersions).

10. WHERE THERE IS A CHOICE TO BE MADE, THERE IS A LESSON TO BE LEARNED.

Always have the courage to act decisively and to assume risk in order to gain experience. Risk-taking raises awareness of one's limitations and capabilities. Not all things in life will be pleasant, but what really matters is what we learn from any given situation. There is value to every experience, so recognize the outcome of your actions, take ownership, learn from it, and move on with life. Good judgment comes from experience, and that sometimes comes from bad judgment.

11. LUCK IS WHEN PREPARATION AND OPPORTUNITY MEET.

When an opportunity presents itself, take it! Always be prepared to perform your assigned duties and be ready to lead those who may not have developed the confidence required for the task. Your leadership may be all they need to perform in an outstanding manner. Make the opportunity count by always springing into action and not being afraid of failure.

12. IMAGE IS A FIRST IMPRESSION; DAILY DEMEANOR IS A LASTING IMPRESSION.

Be sure to always present yourself as a caring professional. Be genuine, be yourself, and be honest. Open up avenues of communication and facilitate for others to do the same. Bipolar leadership IS NOT effective. Ensure your personnel know they will always be dealing with the same person they trust, not the one based on the mood of the day.

13. HEROISM IS OF THE MOMENT, BUT PROFESSIONALISM IS A CONSTANT.

A hero is someone who acts valiantly in the face of danger. A professional is one who always does the right thing, takes time to professionally develop based on organizational needs, and strives for perfection to ensure excellence. Do not confuse the two, because heroes do not always make the best professionals. Also, not all heroes make great leaders. Always measure one's potential by their well-roundedness and potential to serve in a higher grade, not solely on the deeds of the day.

14. LOYALTY IS NOT MINDLESS OBEDIENCE.

Loyalty is the foundation of trust. Trust is built on honesty. Honesty is our best policy. Do not fall victim to following orders that are not clearly understood, immoral, unethical, or just stupid. Have the guts to ask for clarification, provide input as needed, and always stand up for what is right.

15. BAD HABITS ARE LIKE A COMFORTABLE BED: REALLY EASY TO GET INTO AND REALLY HARD TO GET OUT OF.

When it comes to habits, start on the right path early and stay on course for the rest of your military career. Ensure to spot-correct those who are wrong and laud those who are doing right. Always uphold the standards by continuously checking yourself. Get in the habit of leading by example even when you think no one is looking or paying attention . . . because someone always is!

16. A LIFE WITHOUT HUMOR IS LIKE A BOOK WITHOUT WORDS.

Always keep a good sense of humor around the workplace. People tend to do their best work when they are comfortable around their peers and leadership in a welcoming work environment. Have you ever met anyone who doesn't like to have fun and smile? Keep smiling, and show up for duty every day grinning like the Cheshire Cat!

17. KNOW THE DIFFERENCE BETWEEN "CHARACTER" AND "REPUTATION."

Character is who you are; reputation is how others see you. Character is of most importance because it defines you from within. If you have solid character, then your reputation will precede you. The same goes for bad character.

18. A PROMISE MADE IS A PROMISE KEPT.

Promise-keeping is by far one of the most important duties of a leader. Ensure that you do not make promises you are not able to deliver. Take time to research, bring in subject matter experts, develop courses of action, and then inform personnel on what you can do for them (or their organization). Also, be sure to deliver on time.

19. TIME MANAGEMENT IS A WASTE OF TIME. CONCENTRATE ON "ACTION" MANAGEMENT INSTEAD.

Effectively managing five minutes does not give you ten minutes. What you do in those five minutes is what truly matters. Get in the habit of concentrating on actions (to-do list) instead of a clock. Task management will help you maximize the duty day every time.

20. LEAD PEOPLE WITH DIGNITY AND RESPECT AT ALL TIMES.

A fact of life: people will make mistakes. People will also do things that may not match your personal values. They should not be held in contempt because of differences or the negative outcome of a lapse in judgment. Instead, find a way to help them get back on track by first making sure they know what they did wrong in an objective manner, and then help them get out of the hole they got themselves into. "Never leave an airman behind" comes to mind when I think about helping others. Always use dignity and respect, and always take the high road out of any situation. Of note, remember that one should not waste either time or effort on those who are not willing to help themselves first.

(FROM BAF) 23 AUG 09

TRANSCRIPTION OF "TIPS FROM UNCLE RAY"

+ VALUE WHAT YOU DO... EMBRACE IT & EXEL AT IT. IF YOU DON'T, THEN FIND SOMETHING ELSE TO DO
+ ARE YOU COMMITTED TO "MISSION SUCCESS" OR "PERSONAL GLORY"? ALWAYS LOOK AT WHAT YOU ARE DOING, AND THEN WHY YOU ARE DOING IT.
+ ALWAYS HAVE THE ABILITY TO SEPERATE THE 'PEPPER FROM THE FLY SHIT." PAY ATTENTION TO DETAIL.
+ DO NOT THINK THAT GREAT CONFIDENCE CAN COVER UP BULLSHIT. BECAUSE THE END RESULT WILL JUST BE "WELL PRESENTED BULLSHIT". OWN UP TO WHAT YOU DO NOT KNOW & STAY HONEST.
+ CANDID/BLUNT FEEDBACK IS BEST! KNOWLEDGE = POWER & HONESTY = TRUST →

My vision of "carnivore leadership" began to take shape in the writing I did in my Moleskine notebooks nearly two decades ago.

+ STUDY PEOPLE AT ALL LEVELS
- LEARN FROM EVERYONE (GOOD/BAD)
- LEARN FROM LIFE (ITS AN OPEN BOOK)

* MY RECORD IS NOT CLEAN... BUT IT HAS MADE ME A BETTER LEADER & PERSON. I HAVE NOT BEEN SHELTERED FROM THE CHALLENGES THAT LIFE BRINGS US. THE GREAT THING ABOUT THIS IS THAT I CAN NOW HELP OTHERS FROM MAKING SIMILAR MISTAKES & EXPAND ON WHAT HAS WORKED FOR ME. GIVING IS EVERYTHING

+ COMMITMENT & SKILL SET IS THE ESCENCE OF A GREAT MILITARY TROOP. STAY ENGAGED W/ THEM. FACILITATE AND ENABLE THEIR SUCCESS.

+ "NO" SHOULD NEVER BE YOUR FIRST ANSWER. ALWAYS TAKE THE TIME TO LOOK AT ALL POSSIBILITIES WHILE KEEPING A "CAN DO ATTITUDE"

+ NEVER SHUT ANYONE OUT. ALWAYS GIVE EVERYONE A CHANCE TO PRESENT THEIR CONCERNS & RECOMMENDATIONS.

+ BEST POLICY FOR STAYING IN SHAPE IS TO NEVER GET OUT OF SHAPE. DO IT OUT OF SELF-RESPECT & PRESERVATION... NOT JUST TO CHECK A BLOCK. LIVESTRONG!

+ NEVER PASS UP A GREAT OPPORTUNITY TO SHUT THE FUCK UP IF YOU DO NOT HAVE ANYTHING PRODUCTIVE TO SAY

+ GIVE RESPECT TO THOSE WHO DESERVE IT AND NONE TO THOSE WHO DON'T. RESPECT IS EARNED... NEVER GIVEN

+ ALWAYS GIVE MORE THAN WHAT YOU TAKE... YOUR PEOPLE COME FIRST

+ ACCEPT MISTAKES BECAUSE YOU ARE TRYING YOUR HARDEST TO MAKE THINGS HAPPEN, NOT BECAUSE YOU ARE BEING LACKADAISICAL ABOUT YOUR DUTIES. THEN HAVE THE SENSE TO LEARN FROM THOSE MISTAKES AND NEVER REPEAT THEM AGAIN.

+ ALWAYS TELL YOUR LOVED ONES YOU LOVE THEM... THEN KISS & HUG THEM... TODAY MAY BE THE LAST CHANCE YOU GET TO DO SO. →

+ TAKE CARE OF YOUR PEOPLE... THEY WILL IN TURN TAKE CARE OF YOU.

+ REALIZE THAT THERE ARE PEOPLE OUT THERE WHO ARE LOST CAUSES. GIVE EVERYONE A FAIR SHOT BUT DO NOT WASTE TIME HELPING THOSE WHO ARE NOT WILLING TO HELP THEMSELVES.

+ QUALITY CONTROL IS ALWAYS MUCH EASIER AND LESS PAINFUL THAN DAMAGE CONTROL.

+ FAILURE TO LEARN FROM HISTORY'S MOST PAINFUL LESSONS WILL GUARANTEE A REPEAT OF HISTORY'S MOST TRAGIC MISTAKES.

+ THE PATH TO SUCCESS IS NOT EASY, CHEAP, OR QUICK. IT WILL REQUIRE GETTING UP AN HOUR EARLIER & GOING TO BED AN HOUR LATER.

+ IF YOU WANT TO FLY WITH THE EAGLES, DON'T HANG AROUND WITH THE TURKEYS (CZ)

ABOUT THE AUTHOR

RAMÓN COLÓN-LÓPEZ is a veteran who served in the United States Air Force for thirty-three years. In December 2019, he became the fourth Senior Enlisted Advisor to the Chairman (SEAC) of the Joint Chiefs of Staff, the most senior enlisted service member in the US Armed Forces.

Born and raised in Puerto Rico, Colón-López moved to the United States in 1986. After graduating high school, he attended Sacred Heart University in Fairfield, Connecticut, seeking a degree in biology. During his first year in college, he made the decision to enlist in the US Air Force to secure his independence and to gain more discipline and structure in his life. His military trajectory led him to the special operations arena, where he successfully completed some of the most rigorous training the Department of Defense has to offer, including the US Air Force's Pararescue pipeline, Navy SEAL and Army Special Forces courses, and other joint special operations training.

Colón-López was a special operations pararescueman for two decades in combat, with a decade of experience in the Joint

Special Operations Command (JSOC) as a Special Tactics Team Leader, Advanced Force Operations Team Leader, and as the 24th Special Tactics Squadron and 724th Special Tactics Group Senior Enlisted Advisor, working alongside Delta Force and SEAL Team Six during dozens of raids and missions. After his special operations career, he went on to lead at the strategic level in several organizations in the United States, Japan, Qatar, Germany, Africa, and other locations across the globe. Throughout his military career, he interacted with leaders from eighty-nine countries, building alliances and partnerships to enhance global security.

Serving as the SEAC, he led the Department of Defense forces during one of the most difficult times in our nation's recent history. He advised three secretaries of defense and two United States presidents, making critical decisions concerning budgetary, modernization, and recruiting challenges.

As the first airman to hold the SEAC position, Colón-López became the first enlisted member of the US Armed Forces to be awarded the Defense Distinguished Service Medal, the nation's highest non-combat award, for outstanding contributions to national security in a position of great responsibility. He has earned a total of fifty-eight medals, including two Defense Superior Service Medals, the Legion of Merit, the Defense Meritorious Service Medal, and numerous other awards, medals, badges, and honors. During his combat time, he earned two Bronze Star Medals for valor and combat operations and was the US Air Force's first-ever recipient of the Combat Action Medal.

Highlighting an illustrious military career, he was honored in his hometown of Guánica, Puerto Rico, with a namesake road, Carretera SEAC Ramón Colón-López, on Highway 1116. He was also the recipient of the Eurípides Rubio Medal, presented by the Commonwealth of Puerto Rico for an accomplished military career with significant valorous combat actions and honor. Additionally, he was inducted into the Puerto Rico Veterans Hall of Fame, and his combat story is displayed at the US Air Force Museum at Wright Patterson Air Force Base, Ohio, and at the Enlisted Heritage Hall in Montgomery, Alabama. He has also been recognized twice as an "Eagle" by the US Air Force Air Command and Staff College during the Gathering of Eagles program (2013 and 2025) and received the National Defense Industrial Association DeProspero Lifetime Achievement Award for his contributions to national security and special operations.

Colón-López currently serves on the Military Board of Advisors for First Command Financial Services and as an independent strategic consultant for several multimillion-dollar firms, including Atlantic Diving Supply, Inc., Robert Irvine's Warrior Ventures, and the Public Safety Training and Response Group. In addition, he is a member of the Board of Directors for the Robert Irvine Foundation, and volunteers for veteran support and nonprofit organizations.

Colón-López's education includes a bachelor of science degree from the University of Maryland, a National Preparedness Leadership Initiative fellowship at Harvard University, and many other leadership courses at the University of North Carolina, Alan Freed and Associates, the Center for Creative Leadership, and several other military and civilian organizations.

He lives with his wife, Janet, and their rescue dogs, Zephyr and Cairo, in North Carolina and enjoys mountaineering, rock and ice climbing, mountain biking, shooting, and writing in his spare time.

A portion of proceeds from the sale of this book will go to the Robert Irvine Foundation, whose programs support heroes and their families through four initiatives: food, wellness, community, and financial.

Its food programs offer shared meals to promote bonding, address food insecurity, and mentor veteran culinary entrepreneurs.

The wellness programs provide opportunities for healing to address the invisible and visible wounds of our nation's heroes by reconnecting combat units, matching service dogs, and offering adaptive mobility devices.

Its community programs foster connection through resiliency events, education, base visits, and more.

Financial support eases burdens with grants and scholarships for service members, veterans, Gold Star families, and surviving loved ones. Together, these efforts have impacted over one million heroes, their families, and civilians, creating lasting and meaningful change.

LEARN HOW TO GIVE HERE: